THESE ARE NOT GENTLE PEOPLE

Also by Andrew Harding
THE MAYOR OF MOGADISHU (2016)

"Andrew Harding is one of the great foreign correspondents. His book disdains cliché and reductive analysys, in the process creating some of the most beautiful writing about Africa that I have ever seen"
FERGAL KEANE

"Africa can be explained in dry prose, in figures, in newspaper reports; or it can be explained, as Andrew Harding does in this book, through an astonishing personal story, vivid and utterly memorable. This is a triumph of a book: surprising, informative, and humane"
ALEXANDER McCALL SMITH

"A wonderful account of one of the most troubled yet beautiful countries on Earth, told by one of our most gifted and sensitive journalists. This is a book laced with hope amid the dark layers of hatred through which the Mayor of Mogadishu battles"
JON SNOW

"Andrew Harding's elegantly written account is much more than a portrait of the Mayor of Mogadishu. In bold, vivid brush-strokes it captures all the charm, colour, contradiction and menace of contemporary Somalia"
MICHELA WRONG

Andrew Harding

THESE ARE NOT GENTLE PEOPLE

Two dead men. Forty suspects.
The trial that broke a small
South African town

MACLEHOSE PRESS
QUERCUS · LONDON

First published in Great Britain in 2020 by

MacLehose Press
An imprint of Quercus Publishing Ltd
Carmelite House
50 Victoria Embankment
London EC4Y 0DZ

An Hachette UK company

A CIP catalogue record for this book is available
from the British Library.

ISBN (HB) 978 1 52940 558 3
ISBN (TPB) 978 1 52940 559 0
ISBN (Ebook) 978 1 52940 561 3

10 9 8 7 6 5 4 3 2 1

Designed   ugh
Printed a   ).A.

Papers used by Qu   sible sources.

CONTENTS

DRAMATIS PERSONAE

On the farms

The Van der Westhuizens: "Oom" Loedie Senior, his son
Boeta, Boeta's wife Rikki, their children Loedie Junior, Marie,
Crista and her fiancé Miela Janse van Rensburg. Boeta's cousins
Neils and Vicky, Vicky's son Muller, nephews Wian and Wicus,
and farm manager Fanie Oosthuizen, his brother Johann,
Fanie's wife Joelene and their son Daniel. Hector and Mercia.

Their neighbours: Anton Loggenberg, his wife Gusta, and their
son Cor. Johan Cilliers and his son, Johan. Ockert Van Zyl,
Kobus Dannhauser and his farm manager Thomas Direko and
worker Isaac Xhalisa, Pieter Kemp

In the township

Samuel Tjixa, his mother Ruth Qokotha, his girlfriend Naledi,
and his brothers Elias and Lawrence.

Simon Jubeba, his sisters Susan, Dimakatso and Jemina, their
aunt Selina, grandmother Norma, and his friends Richard and
Baba Mbele

In town

Captain Henk Prinsloo, a community police officer, his wife Rona and daughters Arne and Alicia

Colonel Deon Topkin and Captain Francois Laux – Directorate for Priority Crime Investigation, "the Hawks"

Casualty ward Doctor Sifiso Nxumalo

Paramedics David Mongali and Relebone Marosela

Nurses Margaret Mafubelu and Mantoa Lefatle

Paul Thebane – E.F.F. activist

Dominee Ian Jonker

In court

Magistrate Leshni Pillay

Judge Corne Van Zyl

Defence team – Kobus Burger, Barry Roux, Jan Ellis, Nico Dreyer, Hans de Bruin, Dawie Reynecke, Piet Pistorius, Hennie Du Plessis

Prosecution team – J.J. Mlotshwa and Sandile Mtetwa

Court translator – Jeremia Tollie

Dr Buang Lairi – pathologist

Professor Jan Botha – forensic pathologist

Dr Werner van Tonder – trauma surgeon

One year is a year of rain,
Another a year of dryness,
One year the apples are abundant.
Another year the plums are lacking.
Yet we have gone on living,
Living and partly living.

— FROM T.S. ELIOT, "MURDER IN THE CATHEDRAL"

1

LOOK WHAT THE DOGS DID

THEY RAN AS a pack. Sixteen feet pounding and scratching the hard earth, heading south, with the low sun picking them out like a spotlight. Dark silhouettes against the drought-bleached fields.

The white woman saw them first.

They're here. On the farm. They're crossing our land.

She could see five figures, two men and three lanky dogs, perhaps a little over 200 metres away, their long shadows flickering first against a water tank, then slowing and shrinking as the men ducked under a barbed-wire fence.

The woman stood near her small, rundown farmhouse, her back to the motorway and a mobile to her ear. She was a stout, straight-backed, unflappable woman, glad to see the end of this nonsense.

On the phone, she told the others to head towards the clump of bluegums at the southern edge of the property. They could corner them there. And the rest would follow.

Within minutes she saw the dust from two cars begin to converge, and then, as the word spread, more cars, and more clouds of dust turning pale orange in the fading light.

*

Samuel Tjixa watched his friend squeeze under the barbed-wire, then did the same, trying not to tear his dark blue sweater. The dogs made their own way through and soon they were running together again across an empty stretch of grazing land.

It was hard to know if they'd been spotted yet. The old man had warned them there would be a chase. They'd already covered three kilometres since leaving his farm, and it would be the same distance again, further even, to the motorway service station, which was just visible in the distance. So they kept a steady pace, both men panting now, sweat clinging to their hair and darkening the back of Simon Jubeba's orange T-shirt.

As for the old man's dogs – skinny, languid greyhounds – they were just tagging along for the ride. Maybe they'd thought the two visitors were going rabbit hunting when they'd raced off so suddenly. Now they trotted, effortlessly, almost mockingly, alongside their new companions. Simon was a gangly 29-year-old with arched eyebrows, a broad, flat nose, and a slight limp from an old football injury. Samuel was older, darker and slighter, with short dreadlocks.

The group ran, in silence, past a high-sided concrete water tank. They could hear the steady creak of the wind pump and the cry of egrets rising from the pale grass. The tank was overflowing, turning the thirsty earth around it dark and muddy. Ahead was another rusting fence, then the trees, then a gentle slope towards the motorway station.

Suddenly, they heard the sound of a car's engine, revving hard.

In fact, there were two cars bearing down on them. One lurching through the gate in the far corner of the field nearest to the motorway. The other coming from the other direction. The vehicles roared towards them, shuddering across the rutted earth, swerving to avoid termite mounds. The three hunting dogs skipped away as if they had already made other plans, and Simon and Samuel veered apart.

Seconds later, Samuel heard the squeal of brakes, then a door slamming shut, and someone shouting.

The young white farmer was surprised to see the black man stop, almost immediately, and turn towards him. Samuel stood, panting hard, his shoulders slack, no attempt at eye contact, the fight gone out of him.

Fok. O.K. Now sit down. Right now. And put your hands behind your back. Don't you bloody move.

Samuel, used to taking orders, did as the younger man told him.

About thirty metres ahead, Simon was still running towards the fence. If he could get over it, perhaps the cars would have to go the long way around. He still had a chance. The ground became rockier as he charged past the trees. There were rabbit holes, and a few grey logs hiding in the shade. He could hear someone behind him, heavy feet thumping the ground, catching up. Then he felt a powerful blow to his waist and the tight grip of a rugby tackle hurling him forwards and down. A fist smashed into the side of his face. It was over.

Someone sent a text message to tell the others.

We've got the fucking kaffirs.

*

By the time the police arrived, some three hours later, it was properly dark. The officers had driven out on the dirt road from Parys, under the motorway, up onto the faded ridge of an ancient crater, and then turned right at the crossroads beside the cathedral-like grain silos on Weiveld farm. They'd stopped first at Loedie van der Westhuizen's farm, Bulrush, to check in with their colleagues, who were already taking a statement from the old man and examining his injuries.

Then they went searching for the field, got lost, got lost again, eventually spotted a cluster of headlights and turned onto a threadbare pasture dotted with rocks and smooth termite mounds.

A couple of hours earlier the field had been like a carpark. Maybe forty people gathered at the scene – farmers, friends, teenage sons. Now most of them had left, some calling ahead to tell their wives that it was all over, that Oom Loedie would be just fine, and that they'd be back for dinner after all.

The policemen's flashlights picked out the trees, the fence, a few familiar faces, and a white pickup. They walked over and peered into the back of it.

Samuel and Simon were lying clumsily, like drunks sleeping it off. Simon was sprawled near the tailgate with his jeans around his knees, and Samuel in his blue sweater was slumped against the back of the driver's cabin. Both were breathing in shallow, almost panicky gasps. Even in the dark, and with their black skin, you could see the bruising and the swollen faces.

Look what the fucking dogs did to them, someone muttered.

No-one mentioned the rope, or the monkey-wrench, or the gun, or the knife, or the stick, or the whip, or the blood-stained boots. In fact, no-one said much at all. It seemed simpler that way. There was no sense in pointing fingers. The important thing was that the old man was fine.

You say nothing. You know nothing. You do nothing, one father told his son.

The night was warm and windless, with the moon a shrinking crescent. The motorway had fallen silent. The headlights of the last farmer's car strummed the line of trees in the corner of the field, and then locked onto the speckled dust cloud of the departing police van bumping over the rough earth, carrying two limp bodies back to town.

2

BLOOD ON THE WALL

RUTH QOKOTHA HAD been dreaming about money. She
woke early, as usual, just before dawn. A stray gust of
wind tugged at the tin roof of the musty shack she lived in on
La Rochelle farm, east of the Weiveld crossroads. She sat up
in bed.

Soon the first rays of sunlight were peeking inside, warm-
ing the air, revealing cupboards and smoke-stained walls. It
was going to be another scorching day.

She could hear a neighbour opening their door. Probably
Pauline, heading to one of the communal pit latrines out the
back.

Ruth's dream had involved ludicrous mountains of bank
notes and, for some reason, big plates of meat. She shrugged it
off. Her mother had always told her that money dreams meant
bad news – usually a death – but Ruth wasn't inclined to pay
too much attention to that sort of stuff.

She looked at herself in the mirror.

What can I do? I'm ugly.

Ruth had a habit of talking about herself as if she was com-
menting, wryly, on someone else. Someone faintly ludicrous.
Her laugh – throaty and infectious – came easily and lingered.

She would shout at her three boys. Scream at them sometimes. But anger didn't sit well with her.

By seven she'd bathed, eaten, swept the floor, and was on her way to work. Her route took her past a pile of grey logs, three cars under an old tarpaulin, and some rusting electricity pylons. She raised an arm to acknowledge the men setting off towards the farmyard, and followed the dirt road as it curved towards a nearby farmhouse. By the gate a big sign, sponsored by a local fertiliser company, declared that the property, La Rochelle farm, belonged to Hector and Mercia van der Westhuizen.

As she walked across the lawn, a posse of five inquisitive dogs of varying sizes came over, sniffed at her skirt and then wandered away. Ruth had been living on the farm for fourteen years, working as a cleaner, and occasional cook, for Hector and Mercia, and now helping out with their three young children. Before that there had been other farms, and other kitchens.

Always for white bosses. Since from when we were slaves. Hah!

Her husband, Elias, had died two years earlier, from tuberculosis, and drink. They'd had a happy marriage. Right and nice. But in the end the alcohol had made things difficult. For the last years of his life, after he'd lost his job at the oil refinery, he had worked as a garden boy at La Rochelle. She knew 'boy' was a deliberate insult, but it wasn't her language anyway, or Elias', and so they just added it to the pile of words and facts and indignities that mostly seemed easier to shrug off.

For many years, Ruth, Elias, and their three sons, Samuel, Elias and Lawrence, had shared the one-roomed shack at La Rochelle. The boys had attended a school close by and then worked for Hector and his brothers in the fields until, one by one, they'd drifted away to find work, and perhaps the chance of a little privacy, elsewhere.

Ruth pulled on her apron and began her morning chores. She worried about her middle boy, Elias, who had always been the troublemaker – sent home from school again and again, then drinking like his father, and now getting into fights on the farm, in the township taverns, and sometimes with women too. Lawrence was placid, gentle. It was hard to tell what he was thinking most of the time. He was a hard, steady worker, but he suffered from epilepsy and struggled to find jobs. Samuel, tall and lighter skinned like his father, was the best company, always coming home at the weekend with some money for Ruth, and maybe with his girlfriend too – a nice girl, this latest one, perhaps too young, but always helping with the cleaning.

Ruth started, as usual, by making the beds, then sorting and washing clothes. When she was done with that part of her routine, she went into the small, old-fashioned kitchen to prepare lunch. One of the dogs wandered in, looking for scraps. Mercia would be back soon, bringing the older children home from their nursery school in Parys. A sign on the wall read 'Good Mums have Sticky Floors, Dirty Ovens, and Happy Kids!'

*

The road west from La Rochelle followed the old train line back towards town. In places the disused track, warped and dark with age, rose from the surrounding fields like a writhing snake.

At the crossroads, the workshop on Weiveld farm was starting to fill up. By the time Wian van der Westhuizen arrived, his cousins, Wicus and Muller, were already there, and so was Fanie Oosthuizen, the farm manager, and his brother Johann. Wian was a thin young man, twenty years old, with a wispy beard and curly fair hair and, this morning, a slight limp, of which he seemed rather proud. Soon they were all joking about last night.

Fanie had a photograph on his mobile of one of the blacks – the one in the orange T-shirt – lying in the back of the white bakkie.

He looks like he's been run over by a train, Fanie said. He and his brother laughed.

That will confuse the police – if they ever come looking, Fanie went on. After all, where would they find a train, out here, these days?

When the black workers arrived, Wian walked over to boast. He was like that, Fanie thought – a little man with a big mouth. Wian told the men he'd given two thieves a good kicking last night. In fact, they'd danced on them. That would teach them – and anyone else who might be tempted to steal – a good lesson.

No-one messed with the Van der Westhuizens.

They could look at the blood on his shoe if they liked.

*

A few miles south of the crossroads, on Bulrush farm, Oom Loedie was having breakfast with his son and daughter-in-law at the old family dining room table. He was stiff and sore. He had bruises on his stomach, a small cut on his suntanned right forearm, and another cut, covered now by a white bandage, just above his left ear.

Rikki had tried to clean things up last night, but there was still blood on the wall near the panic button.

Time to go, Rikki said. She guided her father-in-law towards the front door. He needed those cuts seen by a doctor in town.

Oom Loedie was a rough, stubborn man – his neighbours called him old-fashioned, and not all of them meant it as a compliment. A widower, he lived alone and he liked it that way, shuffling around the old farmhouse with its brown walls and dark wooden furniture and a metal fence outside that made the place look more like a prison than a home. But these days his arthritis was playing up and, at seventy-three, his heart was giving him trouble too: one valve wasn't closing properly. Rikki and Boeta had slept in the spare room last night, just to keep an eye on him.

As the three of them walked out into the sunshine Oom Loedie stopped.

It was right here, he said.

At around five late the previous afternoon, he'd just got out of his car and was feeding his two dogs when two blacks, or maybe three, had emerged from the shadow of a tree. They were already inside the metal fence. They were wearing handkerchiefs tied over the lower half of their faces, but he could see their eyes, and those eyes seemed full of hate. They wanted money. They had a pistol. They told him to go inside his house.

Your workers say you have money in the safe. We want twenty thousand rand.

It was well known in the neighbourhood that Oom Loedie was rich. He had two thousand head of cattle on his farm and, so the rumour went, a hundred million rand in the bank.

Oom Loedie said the men shoved him towards the door. Beyond it was a second door. He'd opened the first, then tried to slam it shut behind him to escape from the men, but he'd been too slow. That was when one of them had clubbed him on his head with the gun and he'd stumbled. Blood was pouring down his left cheek, onto his chest, and down onto his shorts. But he'd kept ahead of them and turned into the dining room, where he'd slammed his hand against the little white panic button on the wall, sending an immediate alarm signal to the private security company on the main road in town.

Now, he'd said, pausing to catch his breath. Now you boys will have to run. I've pressed the alarm. The others will be here any minute.

And so the two men had run off, through the farmyard, past the big sheds, the combine harvester and the cattle pen, heading south, chased by the dogs, who had quickly caught up with them, scanning the fields ahead for rabbits, joining the adventure.

*

They went to Parys in Boeta's red pickup, Boeta driving, his father beside him, and Rikki in the back seat. They followed the train tracks, swung under the motorway, drove past a half-built chicken abattoir, and then on in the direction of a few wispy clouds of white smoke. It seemed like Boeta was doing 120 kilometres per hour at least, gliding over the ruts and the potholes. Rikki looked out of her window as the familiar scenery flashed past in a blur – the bonfires, the mounds of smoking rubbish close to the road's edge, and small groups of people, hunched over, looking for scraps, combing through the rubbish. And she thought to herself what she always thought at this point on the journey into Parys.

This is what the end of the world will look like.

The evening before, she and Boeta had been at home on their farm, Cook's Rest, just north of the crossroads, when Oom Loedie had called. They'd had friends visiting and the children were elsewhere – their youngest girl, thirteen-year-old Marie, was at a sleep-over. It was still hot and just about everyone was in the swimming pool, Boeta standing in the shallow end with a cold beer in his hand. He was a stout man, with a plain, open face, square-jawed, and his father's long, drooping nose above a mouth that slipped too easily these days into a sneer. Some people said the nose, broken a few years back in a fight, made him look aristocratic. Boeta was many things, Rikki would reply, with her tight smile, but her husband was no aristocrat. These days she spoke of him with an exasperation that hinted at deeper problems in their marriage. At least father and son were getting along better now – the loans, the bankruptcy, the fights more or less forgotten.

At first no-one had wanted to get out of the pool to answer the telephone. It was Boeta who finally went inside and picked up. When he came back out, he was already running, barking the words out like an order.

Oom Loedie. An attack. Two blacks.

*

At nine o'clock the following morning, the manager on duty at the Executive Car Wash on Water Street in Parys watched a prodigiously large man – a farmer, judging by his shorts and checked shirt – haul himself and his stomach out of a white pickup. He asked her to give the vehicle a good clean, particularly the back area, and then headed across the busy road to the Spur family restaurant.

A few moments later, another man drove in. He was tall and wore a black cowboy hat. An eccentric figure. He also wanted his pickup cleaned. He was talkative, and within minutes had taken out his mobile and was showing her some photos.

At first she couldn't make out what she was looking at. A blue and grey diamond pattern, blotches of green and red.

We killed two kaffirs last night, the man said, by way of explanation. And the way he said it, it was almost like he meant it as a pick-up line.

Suddenly the manager could make out the two black men, photographed as they lay in the back of a pickup. She and her husband had both been police officers, back in the good old days, as she sometimes put it, and so she wasn't easily shocked.

But still, to hear a stranger boasting of murder ...

The tall man left his car to be washed and strode across the street to the Spur. He walked inside and spotted his friend, the large man, sitting at a table with two others.

Hello, murderers! he said with a grin.

3

FROZEN

A T NOON, RUTH Qokotha heard her boss, Hector, coming into the house and settling down with his wife in the small T.V. room beside the kitchen to watch the cricket. She took their lunch – curry and rice – through to the dining room and was busy setting the table when her mobile rang in her pocket.

Did you hear? said a woman's voice. It was Ruth's niece, Miriam, calling from Parys.

They say your son and his friend were beaten to death last night.

What? Which son?

Samuel. They say the police beat them.

Ruth put the mobile back in her pocket, set down the jug of water she was holding in her other hand, and crumpled to the floor. Samuel, she thought, her firstborn. For some reason, she pictured him singing in church. A few minutes later, she pulled herself to her feet, her face wet, and her legs wobbling. She went to the T.V. room and stood in the doorway.

Someone phoned me – they say the police hit my son to death, she announced, quietly, then added, almost as a reflex, I'm finished working now.

Mercia gave her husband a meaningful look. Then she stood up, put her two-year-old daughter, Yannika, on her hip, and followed Ruth into the kitchen.

Mercia was thirty-six, with short brown hair, an angular face, a pleasant singsong voice, and a growing sense of unease about the life she'd married into. She'd met Hector when they were both students at the agricultural and hotel school just across the fields beside the Weiveld crossroads.

The Van der Westhuizens were everywhere – Boeta, Vicky, Neils, Wicus, Wian, Oom Loedie, Klein Loedie, Hector, Jacob, Louie – a network of cousins and uncles and grandfathers who appeared to own almost every farm in the district and tended to act accordingly. Hector had no plans, no ambitions, beyond farming. Injuries permitting, he played scrumhalf for a local rugby team alongside Boeta van der Westhuizen, enjoyed a little golf, some hunting and clay pigeon shooting. He attended church in town every Sunday. Hector seemed to amble comfortably through life. Mercia had worked as a florist, then a waitress, and after they were married she settled into her role as a full-time Van der Westhuizen wife and mother.

But life on the farm had begun to change. One morning, a few years back, Hector had been inspecting the cattle on La Rochelle when he'd heard shouts from a small brick house near the road. Someone was waving frantically at him to come over. The house was occupied by an elderly white couple from Pretoria, the Van Rooyens, who had come to spend their retirement running a small tuck-shop for the farmworkers. Anna and Ernst sold cold-drinks, sweets, single cigarettes and basic groceries from the window of an old garage beside the home they were allowed to stay in rent free. Anna was a chatterbox, and Ernst loved to feed his ducks and tell old jokes. Mercia would sometimes stroll along with her children for a chat, and the neighbouring farmers' sons would drop by in their pickups to grab a soda on hot afternoons.

Now Hector approached the main house, warily. The door was bolted, but he could hear the television was on. That made no sense. He pushed a side door open and looked around. The place was empty. He turned around and walked over to the garage, opened the door and saw 76-year-old Ernst lying on the floor beside his counter in a dark pool of blood, with a T-shirt covering his face and what looked like a single stab wound to the heart.

The police arrived from Parys about an hour later, but neither they, nor Hector, nor his brothers, could find 74-year-old Anna. They checked the house again, and then the nearby fields. Nothing. Then one of the policemen returned to the back room of the shop and took a closer look at the big chest freezer where the Van Rooyens kept some meat and a few other provisions. He found Anna buried under the meat. Someone had stabbed her half a dozen times, wrapped barbed-wire around her neck, and then poured soft drink over her, as she lay, still alive – as the autopsy would later reveal – in the bottom of the freezer.

Ernst used to keep the cash in a small bag hanging on a nail on the back of the same freezer. The robbers didn't find it. It was a poorly planned crime. Some of the farmworkers had seen one of the men walking near the house the evening before and had recognised him as someone who had left the farm two years earlier after a dispute about money. The police found him in a nearby township and tracked down his accomplice soon afterwards.

The killings had hit Mercia hard. She took to wearing two panic buttons on a chain around her neck, linked by radio to a security company in Parys. And she began to wonder about the other workers still living on the farm – about what they might be capable of. Maybe it was time to abandon the farm, and South Africa, and follow the example of her nephew who had just moved his family to New Zealand.

We can't live like this anymore, she'd said to her husband one lunchtime. I don't see any future. It's not going to get any better. I just want to go to a place where it's safe for the children – where I know they'll have a future.

Hector had nodded, but then he had thought about the farm, and his brothers, and his grandfather's grave, and no more was said about it.

But the memory of the Van Rooyens haunted all the farms in the region. Not just the killings, but that sight of the police van driving away with the couple's freezer tied down in the back. The soft drink had frozen around Anna's body, making it impossible to remove, so they'd carried her away still trapped inside the freezer, bumping along the dirt road, past the grain silos, into Parys.

Even now, whenever she thought about it, Mercia's hand would rise, unbidden, to stroke one of the panic buttons near her throat.

*

Ruth and Mercia stood, awkwardly, in the kitchen. Although she hadn't mentioned it yet, Mercia had heard about the incident last night. Hector was on the local farmers' WhatsApp security group, and had received an alert message around six, warning that Oom Loedie had been attacked.

He had rushed to his pickup and driven straight to Bulrush farm, thinking, like his wife, about the chest freezer on the back of that police van. Wondering what someone had now done to his uncle.

In fact, the old man had seemed fine. Shaken, for sure, and with blood caked to his shoulder and stomach, but determined not to appear weak in front of his relatives, or the two policemen who had arrived at his house. Hector had stayed for twenty minutes and then driven back home to his family, deciding not to join the manhunt in the fields further south.

Thank God I didn't go there, he would say to Mercia, more than once, in the months that followed.

Hector had heard a few names being mentioned in connection with the incident. One was Tjixa. He wondered if Ruth's second son, Elias, might have been involved. It wouldn't have been a surprise. Elias had worked for Hector in the past. He was lazy. Too fond of drink, just like his father, and quick to get in fights. And there was the time Elias had tried to organise a strike, demanding more than the one thousand five hundred rand in wages that he and his co-workers were paid each month, and no more working on Saturdays. A troublemaker.

Mercia had also assumed it would be Elias. It made sense. Unlike his tall, easy-going older brother Samuel, Elias had always been difficult. Not exactly a gangster. But not someone to trust either. They'd been glad when he'd finally left their farm of his own accord a few years ago.

In the kitchen, Mercia, still bouncing Yannika on her hip, stood facing Ruth, a woman twenty years her senior, who stood, sobbing hard, with her back to the fridge.

Who did that to your child? Mercia asked.

Ruth shook her head.

We heard that one of your sons was involved in a farm attack.

Mercia still assumed it was Elias.

Ruth said nothing, just stood.

Then Hector appeared at the kitchen door and said that he, too, had heard about the farm attack.

There was another awkward pause.

The couple felt they were playing it straight. They'd heard gossip about the attack, and the possibility that one of Ruth's sons had been involved, and injured, or possibly even killed. But it wouldn't have been fair of them to share this with Ruth – to worry her unnecessarily – until they knew the details for sure. They were just trying to be good employers in a country where race, and wealth, and language, and history made everything like this so damned complicated.

Ruth heard an entirely different conversation.

As she watched Mercia bouncing Yannika on her hip – an entirely natural movement which now seemed somehow disdainful to her – a blaze of anger tore through her.

Madam had known.

All morning Mercia had known her housekeeper's son was dead. They both did – husband and wife. And what had they done? Watched television. And now they were standing in front of her, so casual, so relaxed, so superior. It seemed impossible to Ruth that someone could be aware of something, anything, as important as this, and not even mention it. That was not the world she'd grown up in, where any news – big or small – was always shared.

And so Ruth seized hold of the only conclusion that made sense to her. The white people were lying. They were protecting their kind. They were in on it.

They must think I'm so stupid, she thought to herself.

Were you there? she asked. She meant where Samuel had died.

Two heads shook solemnly.

No? So, you and me, we know nothing. NOTHING!

It was the first time Ruth had ever spoken in anger to her employers, and habit soon prompted her to back down. She told them she would go into Parys to find out more.

Keep us informed, Hector said.

Ruth could not get out of the house fast enough. She walked back across the lawn, ignoring the dogs snapping at her heels, and turned right, back along the road towards her shack.

*

When Boeta, Rikki and Oom Loedie arrived back at Bulrush farm after seeing the doctor in Parys, they found an unexpected reception – half a dozen police vehicles were parked in the yard.

Overnight the officers' attitude had changed. Now they were stiff and aggressive. They demanded to speak to the old man again.

While Rikki was arguing with them, insisting Oom Loedie needed to rest, telling them to come back tomorrow, and call first, please, Boeta's lawyer telephoned.

Listen, he said. Bad news. It's official, the two blacks are dead. Yes, both of them.

4

CRATER'S EDGE

THE NEXT DAY was a Friday. Ruth had hardly slept. Around three in the morning, she got up, filled an old plastic bottle with water, and set off in the dark to walk the twenty-eight kilometres to Parys. She'd started the journey the previous afternoon, but too late, and no-one had stopped to give her a lift so she'd returned home on foot. Now she was determined. She strode along beside the old railway tracks, listening to the birdsong, as dawn caught up with her, her long shadow pointed towards town.

For the first hour or so, the road was flat. But then it rose, dipped and gently skirted around the side of a small dam, whose silky surface was broken by an old grey tree stump. The dam reflected the tips of the evergreens behind it. Beyond them, to the north-west, Ruth could see the land curving upwards towards a distant line of dark blue hills that hugged the horizon like an oncoming rainstorm.

Two billion years ago, a meteorite the size of a mountain had punched a giant hole in the earth here. It was among the biggest collisions the planet would ever experience. The faded remains of the crater's perfect rim are still visible from space, like a smudge on a beer mat, with a rippling crescent of hills to the north and west, and Parys now near its centre.

Ruth had never heard of the ancient crater, so she would not have known that her son had been attacked on the undulating fields that marked its eastern rim. She walked on for at least three more hours, past farms with names like Graspan, Claasens Rust, Issy and Vrede, before a farmer's pickup finally stopped. She jumped in the back. That was usually the rule. And a few minutes later she was in the centre of town and walking hesitantly into the police station.

They say my son was killed by your men.

No, mama, it was the farmers.

The officer told her to try at the courthouse next door and, by chance, she was just in time.

A slim Indian woman was taking her seat on the raised platform in Courtroom One.

It was 10.30 a.m. on January 8, 2016.

*

Magistrate Leshni Pillay picked up her pen with a flourish, gold bangles jangling on her bare arms, and looked down at the four well-fed men who were now standing, behind their lawyers, in the dock.

She'd been told bail would be a formality. The state wasn't planning to oppose it.

There's a chance, Pillay thought, that we can deal with it quickly, this morning, before it gets into the newspapers and becomes that thing. The thing she dreaded.

She'd been worrying about it since yesterday. How could she not?

Half an hour earlier she'd sent a text message to her boss in Kroonstad, and then called him.

Please, I don't want to do this case, she'd said firmly. I know this town. I live here. It's toxic. It's going to become political.

And then she'd said what she really meant.

It's going to become a race thing.

Now the four accused stood silently before her, like a row of overgrown schoolboys in their shorts and short-sleeved shirts, big hands clasped, respectfully, beneath an undulating range of stomachs.

Pillay recognised accused number 1. Boeta van der Westhuizen had had a few run-ins over the years – fights in town, drunk driving, an incident with some electrical cables. She didn't recognise the next two, a father and son – the Cilliers – who owned the farm near where the dead men had been caught. Accused number 4 was another troublemaker like Boeta. In fact the two were old friends. Anton Loggenberg. He was standing outside the dock, too big to squeeze in beside the others.

The police had telephoned all four of the men on Thursday afternoon and asked them to come to the station as soon as possible. They'd been the first two on the scene, and the last two to leave. It made sense for them to make statements, so they'd gone in willingly. After all, they had nothing to hide. The real crime was a savage farm attack – the attempted robbery of a vulnerable old man.

But within minutes of presenting themselves at the station, the four farmers were put under arrest. It was an outrage.

And now here they were, unshaven and unkempt after a night in the crowded cells behind the courtroom. But it would be sorted out soon enough. Their lawyers had told them bail was a formality. This whole thing was ridiculous.

The courtroom was full. The accused's families sat behind the dock, surrounded by other families waiting for other cases.

The prosecutor, a young black lawyer from Bloemfontein named Sandile Mtetwa, was on his feet.

"My Lady."

"Your Worship," Pillay corrected him sharply. "You will address me as 'Your Worship'."

There was something in his manner that immediately irked her.

"Your Worship," the prosecutor repeated with a glint of sarcasm. "The state opposes bail."

Eyes blinked sharply in the dock. The farmers' lawyers shook their heads in open contempt as the prosecutor explained that the state intended to charge all four accused with premeditated murder.

Magistrate Pillay struggled to hide her own irritation, which only grew as the prosecution and the investigating officer conceded that they had no statements implicating the four. No eyewitnesses. No evidence to speak of. Pillay scratched furiously at a notepad, then lifted her hand above her head, an extravagant gesture, to rest it. She shook her head. The state's case was an insult to the court. They had absolutely no grounds to oppose bail. At least not yet. It had to be a political ploy, a sign of what was to come.

The accused got to their feet again as they watched the

magistrate disappear into her office. They would have to spend the weekend in the cells.

*

Back in her small office, Pillay noticed that the air-conditioner was still broken. The dry summer heat was already bouncing off the high walls. She thought of Durban, of the lazy, humid seaside summers of her childhood. She thought of the twists that had brought her halfway across the country, eight years earlier, to a farming community that still couldn't work out whether to cherish her or chase her out of town.

Pillay was twenty-nine years old when she was appointed to Parys as the new magistrate. She came from an energetic family and had been an ambitious student, fired up, like so many of her colleagues, by the promise of post-apartheid South Africa, and not unduly surprised when she became the first, and youngest, in her class to get promoted. She knew she'd earned it.

She had never heard of Parys before coming here, nor set foot anywhere in the Free State. During the apartheid era people like her – people of Indian heritage – had not been allowed to live there, on the high, farming plateau in the centre of the country, a place set aside, primarily, for Afrikaners and their workers. The flat lands.

On her first day in the job, walking in through the doors of the courthouse, taking in the freshly painted walls, the faint smell of disinfectant, the high ceiling in the airy reception, she'd started to notice, and to make sense of, the frozen, startled faces.

Little black girl. Coolie. Bloody affirmative action.

It was as though she could hear their thoughts; as though she had walked onto some old-fashioned film set; a place so at odds with her world and her life back in Durban that she'd almost laughed. Backs were turned on her. Prosecutors refused to work in her native English. Afrikaans interpreters and clerks were urged to complain about her. Smug white lawyers told her, to her face, that she was an embarrassment, incompetent. In her first week, one man primly informed her: the Department of Justice has done you a disservice appointing you to an Afrikaans town.

Pillay had arrived with a husband, one young daughter, and another on the way. But as the months slipped by she'd noticed that her husband, an Indian like her, who'd worked for her father's business in Durban and happily cooked every evening for the family, seemed to struggle with her new job, her status, and her long hours in the courthouse. They fought. He called his mother-in-law back on the coast to complain that his wife had changed. Pillay bought a new house in Parys with her own money, and without his blessing. They went to see a marriage counsellor. Things got worse.

Maybe God didn't want me to be a mother, she sometimes thought to herself as the years went by. The court consumed her. It meant more to her than coming home early to see her daughters' latest drawings or picking the girls up from school or cooking a family meal.

The moment she'd noticed those judgmental faces in the courthouse, she had decided that Parys would not intimidate her, that she would work seven days a week, and to hell with them all. It wasn't really a decision – she had always been that way. And before a year had passed she noted, with satisfaction, that she was making headway with her sceptical staff, even with the lawyers, and especially with the black community, whose troubles dominated her schedule and filled the court benches and the echoing waiting room every morning.

Marijuana possession, petty theft, fights, rape, domestic violence.

And more than a few murders.

*

Ruth Qokotha took a seat on a wooden bench right at the back of the courtroom. She struggled to hear what the Indian woman was saying. She stared hard at the four men, wishing they would notice her, wanting to shout out.

Afterwards, she walked into the tree-lined yard outside. Two journalists came over and asked her if she was a relative.

"My son was murdered in cold blood," she told them.

And because it was fresh in her mind, because she had not yet seen her son's body – had no idea where he was – because it had stung so much, because no-one had bothered to tell her anything about her boy, she talked, in a fury, not about the killings, or the four men in court, but about Hector van der Westhuizen. About how her boss had kept it all a secret, about how he and his wife had known – must have known – all along.

'I cannot work for my enemy,' Ruth declared.

Afterwards, rather than walking back to the farm, she set

off through Parys towards the township of Tumahole, which was where her boys usually stayed.

Ruth did not consider turning right as she stepped out of the courthouse. Right would have taken her into Bree Street, and into an unfamiliar world – a modern, English-speaking, tourist town, conveniently located just an hour's drive from Johannesburg. The town had its own airstrip and offered tandem skydiving trips over the crater, zip-line adventures, wildlife sanctuaries, retirement homes, golf courses, a range of hotels and something called Stonehenge in Africa – a conference centre distinguished by a few tall blocks of local granite cemented together. All were situated near the banks of the wide, unpredictable Vaal River that flowed from the highlands of Lesotho, through a break in the crater's rim, and along the northern edge of Parys, where its boulder-strewn rapids were a favourite with rafting and canoeing adventure companies.

Instead, Ruth turned left. This took her into the original Parys, an Afrikaans town of gabled homes and white-washed churches. She walked past the town hall, an ironmonger, and a bank, and crossed Kerk Street, Loop Street and Schilbach Street. This Parys was founded in 1873, when a wandering delegation of Afrikaner church elders saw the fords across the Vaal River, the promising farmland, the proximity to Johannesburg and its new gold rush, and decided to build a church there. According to some, the name Parys comes from an abbreviation of Paradise. But today most locals have settled on a more romantic theory – that a visiting German surveyor with a penchant for bestowing European names on the African countryside looked at the river, with its islands, and at the neatly arranged streets of the small town, and decided it bore a charming resemblance to Paris, France.

Ruth reached a wide strip of open land where the old railway line from the farms used to run. She crossed a bridge, then passed more fields, a narrow strip of warehouses and run-down factories, and finally reached the outskirts of Tumahole or, as its residents called it, the location.

The gap between Parys and Tumahole was not accidental. Back in 1912, white townsmen were already writing to the local council to complain that "blacks and whites were mixing along the river banks". Worse still, according to an outraged Mr Angel, "blacks were stretching themselves out on the grass without any consideration for the whites", making remarks "in their own language" about the white bathers and creating "a bad smell". "Decent tourists," he said, "could find nowhere to sit." The mayor asked the police to intervene, and before long, blacks were barred from swimming in the river within the town. Stricter segregation soon followed.

It took Ruth perhaps half an hour to reach the outskirts of Tumahole and the first small brick homes that clustered together on plots a fraction of the size of those in Parys. She turned left at the bus station and walked past the football stadium, a big secondary school, and on up a treeless hillside. On the brow of the hill, the formal houses and roads came to an end, and a strip of homemade tin shacks curved around the outer edge of the township, as if it had sprung a leak.

From here Ruth had the clearest view, to the north, of Parys' competing, segregated identities, framed by the crater's crescent of bluish hills. There was the strip of trees marking the river and broken by the roofs of expensive retirement homes and villas. Below it was the narrow corridor of the tourist town clustered along Bree Street. Then came the old Afrikaner dorp, the strip of no man's land, the township, and the informal settlement itself. As she turned to the south, she could see the smoke and gloom of the open rubbish dump and behind it the vast fields of the commercial farms that stretched to the horizon and far beyond.

5

A FRESH START

THE WEEK BEFORE his death, Samuel Tjixa lay on his girlfriend's bed in Winnie, the informal settlement on the edge of Tumahole, staring at the rusty corrugated-iron sheets above his head, his long legs dangling over the edge of the mattress. It was early on New Year's Day, 2016, and outside he could hear the sounds of neighbours stirring in their own makeshift homes. A plastic bucket slowly filling up at the communal tap. Someone tripping over empty beer bottles on the path between the shacks. The muffled rumble of a pickup tearing past along the dirt road heading out to the farms.

I must get money, Samuel said, as if the thought had been nagging at him for some time. He switched on the radio, looking for a reggae tune.

Beside him, her warm neck resting on his arm, Naledi remained silent, as she so often did, while Samuel began to speak of the wages he was owed – by Boeta van der Westhuizen, and by another man too – and about how he would no longer work for them on the farms, about how he wanted a fresh start, wanted a new job, badly needed the money he was owed.

That Samuel was owed money came as news to Naledi. She was seventeen and still a little overwhelmed by her relationship with a man twice her age, this tall, cheerful, generous man who bought her clothes and food and took her drinking at the weekend with his friends, out in the farms, beyond the grain silos. She was his girlfriend. Together and serious. Everyone knew of it and spoke of it, and she loved him. The youngest of three sisters, Naledi was a quiet, sturdy, good-natured teenager with large almond eyes that turned up enquiringly at the corners. She'd dropped out of school nearly three years earlier after giving birth to a son, Kamohelo, who now lived with her mother in Tumahole, in an area called Mandela. All the neighbourhoods in the township were named after famous people – Winnie, Tambo, Zuma. Her father, a wiry, haunting figure, who'd lost his left eye in a mugging, had simply wandered off one day to another township. Naledi had first met Samuel about two years ago when he was strolling past her one-room shack one afternoon on his way to his own, almost identical shack, a few hundred metres away.

There were worse places to live – townships far more notorious for gangs and rapes – but Naledi still felt vulnerable living alone. She worried that the padlock she had on her door wasn't enough to protect her few belongings; she worried about kids stealing her zinc – the scavenged tin walls and roof of her shack – to sell to the scrap-metal merchants for drug money; she worried about someone following her home in the evening. It helped that everyone knew she was with Samuel now.

Naledi had applied for a social grant, for her boy, worth three hundred and fifty rand a month, but it still hadn't come. She had tried to find work on the farms, without success. For now, she felt she had little choice but to stick with her regular job. She spent her days just a few yards from her shack, beside the dirt road, bent double with her neighbours on the rubbish dump, picking out the bottles and cans and plastic and metal. If she was diligent, and lucky, she could make fifty rand a day selling the scrap to the merchants in town. But it was filthy work, moving among the pigs and cows that foraged among the same scraps, watching out for the rats, and for shards of glass or metal, and the nappies. Occasionally, one of the big pickups that raced past, chased by their own whirlwinds of dust, would stop and offload something worthwhile. Sometimes the abattoir sent a truckload of waste. The refuse bags from the golf estate – a distant green smudge near the river – were highly prized, but the men at the dump would shove and compete for those, and so Naledi would sit, shading herself from the sun with a piece of cardboard, until things calmed down and she could return to pick through a less coveted patch, away from the smoky fires that could hide for days in the dump before springing back to life.

At this time of year, summer rainstorms usually kept the dust and the fires in check. But the drought, the heat, and the swirling winds meant Naledi now returned home every afternoon even more clammy with sweat and grime than usual, and anxious to clean herself. She would fetch water from the communal tap, heat it on a kerosene stove in the shack, and then crouch over a plastic bucket on the small patch of dirt floor beside her bed.

Samuel was drinking a lot. More than usual, even for the holiday season. He didn't tell Naledi much about his work on the farms but she knew his best friend, Simon – the man he stood with at dawn by the road, waiting to be collected to go out to work on the farms – was having difficulties. They'd all been sitting on crates outside the tavern late in the afternoon a few days ago – Samuel, Simon, Naledi, Samuel's younger brother Elias, and another good friend, Richard – and Simon had kept talking about Boeta van der Westhuizen, about something that had happened a few weeks ago on his farm.

Simon was a quiet man until he had a couple of beers inside him. Then he would start doing imitations of the farmers. When he did Boeta's heavy, bow-legged walk, clenching his fist and swearing, he had his co-workers crying with laughter. Ag, man! Fokof! I'll klap you one. I'll moer you!

Eish, that man, Simon said, swigging from a bottle of beer. And he started retelling the tale of the stolen sausages, and the trouble that had followed. The story grew in the telling and before long the others were joining in, offering their own stories about Boeta. Or Boetaki, as they called him. About one time Boeta's dog had fallen into the swimming pool at his house. He got mad, told them they were idiots, that they should have been looking out for the dog – which survived, of course.

He would klap you so hard, Samuel said, nodding. He had stopped working for Boeta more than a month ago and was owed – he insisted – a month's wages. He went up the road to work on another Van der Westhuizen farm, but quit that job too when he felt insulted by the white manager who accused him of driving a tractor too fast. Samuel seemed to have less patience for all that nonsense these days. He was sick of it.

Elias mentioned the worker who'd died, from an electric shock, on Boetaki's farm a while back, after being ordered to

climb up a pylon and reconnect a cable that had been discon-
nected for non-payment. Everyone nodded. Then there was
that white lady in her car who'd been killed when Boeta –
drunk, people said, on brandy – had driven into her on the
edge of town. And Richard had his own story about being
assaulted by Boeta, a black guard and another white man,
maybe four years earlier.

Eish. That man.

Yoh!

But this time, Simon said, returning to the story of the
stolen sausages, he was really mad.

Boeta had accused him and another worker, nicknamed
Stongo, of stealing five big packets of sausage meat each. And
it was true, they had taken the meat from one of the barns
and put it in their bags, and one of the other workers had
gone and told Boeta's son, Klein Loedie. Klein Loedie, a short,
fair-haired, impulsive eighteen-year-old, immediately told his
father, who had come charging out, holding up the bags, pulling out the sausages and shouting at the workers.

You don't know me very well, but you'll know me from
now on, Boeta warned menacingly.

And then he began hitting them. Hard slaps across the face.
Then punches. Everyone saw it. Even Boeta's wife Rikki saw
it, and was not surprised.

But it wasn't stealing, Simon told his friends.

He claimed that Boeta had not paid them at month end, had
told them he was short of cash and would pay them soon,
had made up all sorts of nonsense. Something about a trip
to Johannesburg. And so it was only fair that they take the

sausages. Why not? And the way Simon told it now, it wasn't just a few punches that Boeta handed out – he went crazy, fetched his gun from the house and shot it over their heads as they ran into the undergrowth worrying that the dogs would come after them too.

Simon was drunk as he told the story again. They were all a little drunk. He did a few more of his imitations to make his friends laugh. But there was a deep, brooding anger in Simon's eyes. Richard had seen it once or twice before – it was like a switch had been flipped.

Not long after the sausages incident, Simon's mother died, and he needed money to help pay for the funeral. He asked Elias if he could talk to Boeta about contributing something.

Don't talk to me about that man. Never again. He's a thief, Boeta told Elias.

And just now Simon had broken a window at his family's house, a two-bedroom brick home on the edge of Tumahole, near Naledi's shack. A stupid window. He'd kicked an old football through it when they were playing around in the yard, and now he had to find the money to fix that too.

It was a bad way to end the year. Holiday season, and Simon was jobless and bitter, ground down by life. He and Samuel began making a plan. They would go out to the farms and get the money, the wages, they were owed. At least a month's pay, two thousand rand each. It was only fair. If Boeta didn't have the money, maybe his father, Oom Loedie, would pay up. Boeta often took them to work over there, on Bulrush farm, and everyone knew the old man was fabulously rich. He had huge tractors sitting idle in his sheds. They would go and confront them in the daytime – not like the robbers, not like tsotsis who worked at night. Then, when they'd got the money that was owed to them, they could make a fresh start somewhere else – there was talk of an opportunity in Sasolburg – or maybe go back later and ask for their old jobs back.

None of this was a secret. They told all their friends about it, and Samuel's brother, Elias, said he'd come along too.

Eish, that Boeta.

Boetaki.

*

In bed on New Year's morning, Naledi listened to Samuel talk about the plan, and about getting a driver's licence afterwards. A fresh start. Naledi didn't know what to think. She had a nagging worry that Simon was a bad influence on Samuel – that maybe there was more to this plan than just asking for cash. She sank deeper into silence.

The next afternoon Naledi left Tumahole, hitching a ride to visit a friend who was working on a farm north of Parys. She planned to stay a week or so. It wasn't until 5.00 p.m. on Wednesday, January 6, that she tried calling Samuel on his mobile. It rang a couple of times, then Samuel hung up without answering. She called again and it went straight to voicemail. Then she hung up, unaware that at that exact moment Samuel and Simon were standing in the shade, just outside Boeta's father's house – old man Loedie's place – watching him drive slowly towards them through the fields.

Naledi didn't find out what had happened until Friday, when

Elias called her. He was talking quickly and she didn't hear it properly at first. Something about how Elias should have been with them but had injured his knee and so had gone that morning into Parys, to the hospital, instead.

The dead are no longer with us, Elias said, his voice suddenly clear.

Samuel is dead. Simon too.

Naledi thought he was joking, that Samuel was playing a trick on her to make her come back home early. It was the kind of thing he would do. She hung up and left a message on Samuel's mobile. On Sunday she finally came back to Tumahole, and as she walked through the township she could feel her worries suddenly nipping at her heels, a sense of dread in her chest. She went straight to the shack where she knew Elias often stayed.

What you told me on the phone. Is it true?

Elias was lying in the dark on an old mattress. It is true, he said.

O.K.

Naledi didn't know what to do. She'd been afraid of the police ever since an officer had slapped her when she was ten years old. She had no idea who else to ask, or how to find out what was going on. She did not know about going to court. She went home to her shack, undid the padlock, and lay down on the bed.

6

MONSTERISM

MAGISTRATE PILLAY WAS pushing her trolley past the vegetable counters in Checkers supermarket, one block up from the courthouse, when she noticed that something had changed. She was with her older daughter, Larisa. These days, everyone in town knew their magistrate, and a weekend shopping trip invariably turned into a procession of nods and handshakes and greetings from a white community which had, in recent years, come to accept this young Indian woman as part of the furniture.

But today was different. She was sure she wasn't imagining it. Eyes were averted. Trolleys sidled to other aisles. She could feel a bubble of judgmental silence enveloping her, like it had on her first day at the courthouse eight years ago. She knew it was about this business out on the farms. The town was taking sides.

She remembered an incident from a few weeks earlier, when she'd been woken in the morning by shouting on the street outside and had walked out in her nightgown to find two white men beating a black man. She'd screamed at them to stop.

How dare you. You have no right to beat this man.

The men had muttered something about him being a burglar.

In that case you must call the police.

But the men seemed drunk and Pillay wondered if the black man had just walked in front of their car. Either way, there it was, inescapably, on a quiet suburban street, at six in the morning – this instinct to punish, to klap the blacks.

Now two men were dead, and Pillay was pushing her trolley to the car in angry silence.

This was, she thought, a very, very, very racist town.

Three years earlier, someone had sent her an anonymous bouquet of flowers, and her husband had accused her of having an affair. They'd fought, and when she'd scratched his face he'd reported her to the police. They were divorced soon afterwards. Now she had a new boyfriend, a white man, an Afrikaner with his own plumbing and decorating business in another town. He had spotted Leshni in court one morning and decided she was the most beautiful woman he'd ever seen. He broke up with his fiancée, wrote Leshni an ardent letter, wooed her over coffee, and soon they were living together, with her daughters, at his home in the same residential neighbourhood, near Parys Hospital.

He was the opposite of Leshni; quiet, self-contained, and content to shrug off the taunts and insults that other Afrikaners threw at him when they heard he was dating a coolie. Leshni loved that about him – that and the fact that he didn't watch rugby, or obsess about Afrikaans music or movies, or braaiing, or any of the other defining traits of so many of the white men in this town.

When Leshni returned from the supermarket, he told her to stand her ground.

Just do your job. Don't give a fuck about other people and what they say.

*

In Tumahole, Ruth was feeling much better. For days she'd been sleeping on a relative's floor, worrying about how she could possibly pay for Samuel's funeral. She had an urge, an impatience, to be done with it all, to put her boy to rest, see those four convicted, and set her world back in order.

Quick-quick, she would often say, under her breath as she moved from one task to the next.

Then the local branch of the A.N.C. stepped in. They bought her pilchards, toothpaste and other supplies to see her through the week. They also paid for a cow to be slaughtered at the abattoir, and took care of some other arrangements for the funeral, hiring a local hall near the bus station for the speeches, promising to arrange transport, flowers, everything.

And now here she was, watching four buckets of meat stewing in a big pot outside the hall. People had come from as far away as Sasolburg to pay their respects. Ruth wore a dark skirt and black shirt. She shook hands, and watched the meat being served out. It felt proper. Respectful.

There had been talk of a joint funeral for Samuel and Simon. Which made sense to Ruth. But then things got complicated. In the months before his death Simon had become friends with members of the Economic Freedom Fighters, with their red berets and T-shirts, their cheerful cries of Salut! and constant complaints about the A.N.C. councillors in Tumahole.

Corrupt scum, the E.F.F. called them. They would sit in the front room of Simon's family's home at weekends, railing against President Zuma and against the local deals and contracts that always ended up in the pockets of a few well-connected, A.N.C.-friendly businessmen. The E.F.F. guys were the township's outsiders – indignant, ambitious, unemployed and desperate for a slice of the pie.

Now that Simon was dead, they were practically camped out at his home, up near the rubbish dump, offering to pay for the funeral, determined that the A.N.C. would not muscle in on both grieving families.

A black person's life is cheap, even in his own country, declared a man named Paul, who used to sell soft drinks on the street.

Paul was now the E.F.F.'s local organiser, a garrulous figure with spectacularly crooked teeth, a thin moustache draped over his upper lip, and an old tattoo on his right arm that read "sun of the time" – a phrase he realised he could no longer quite explain.

We want to see consequences. Every time a black person is killed, there is an apology. Nothing more. Apartheid has created monsterism, Paul declared to no-one in particular, savouring the homemade word, and looking around Simon's cramped bungalow. There were steel grilles on the windows, graffiti on the bare walls, and one of those trick photographs of Mandela that changed as you walked round the room. A delicate piece of white crocheting covered the sofa from where Paul was holding forth, talking about how the E.F.F. would even adopt Simon's young daughter, who lived out on the farms with her mother. He had plans for cleaning up the rubbish dump too – maybe forming a workers' association. Paul seemed to be trying to get the attention of Simon's visibly pregnant older sister, Susan, who was standing by the front door.

Susan had taken Simon's death the hardest in her family. Or it seemed that way to her. As kids, one year apart and unable to go to school because their mother had no ID papers, they'd spent most of their time together. Simon had taught her how to use a slingshot to hit birds, and she'd shown him how to play diketo – a game of dexterity involving scooping stones from small hollows in the ground. They had different fathers. In fact their mother had had children with four different men who had all drifted away into the farmlands. But Simon had always been her favourite brother. Sometimes he would joke about becoming a policeman, or a teacher, so he could come back home and pretend to discipline his sisters. He could be properly strict. But mostly he was quiet. Quiet, introverted Simon, and his best friend Samuel, who was always coming round, turning the music up, and making everyone smile – even Norma, Simon and Susan's grandmother, who'd raised them and all the other Jubeba children, and who now sat on a dirty mattress in the backroom, no longer able to talk, or walk, after suffering a severe stroke two years earlier. Norma waved her hand feebly. A pile of adult nappies waited on the windowsill. Beside her, flies covered a homemade cigarette, and a small patch of vomit. Susan knew all about Boeta. Boetaki. And not just how he'd beaten Simon up. She used to have a cleaning job on a nearby farm and knew you couldn't walk past Boeta's place after

6.00 p.m. because he'd let the dogs out if he heard a noise. Everyone knew that. It was just one of those things.

Simon and Samuel's families, and their rival political sponsors, held separate wakes on either side of Tumahole. A big crowd – maybe a hundred people – gathered in the dark by the Jubebas' home. Simon's father showed up. The E.F.F. paid for some food, helped to bring the coffin from the mortuary in Sasolburg, and made more speeches than some people would have liked.

Salut! Paul said. We have taken sworn oaths to follow this case until the end. We hear there were maybe fifty farmers there. They must all be arrested.

Heads nodded. One of the family asked Simon's friend, Richard, who lived next door and worked as an occasional security guard at the golf estate, to say a few words.

I did not expect to lose him, Richard said quietly, rubbing a hand over his close-cropped hair. Not like this. He was my only friend. He was good to me. A good footballer. I hope those guys will pay for whatever they've done. I hear they say he went to do a robbery. That's a lie. He told me he was going to fetch his wages, to ask for two thousand rand. What kind of robber goes there to do his business in the daytime?

In the town hall, a couple of kilometres to the west, A.N.C. councillors called for calm, and urged any farmworkers who knew about the killings to come forward and talk to the police.

Ruth began to grow tired of listening to all the long speeches. Elias and Lawrence stood beside her in their best clothes, slack-shouldered and uncomfortable. Lawrence had hardly spoken in days. Ruth could not get the picture of Samuel out of her head now. All three of them had been to see him, first in the mortuary in Sasolburg and then in a funeral parlour in Parys, after the authorities had brought him back from his autopsy in faraway Bloemfontein. His dark skin was grey and unnatural, ribs broken, his face lumpy and misshapen as if lazily moulded from clay. Ruth had felt an urge to touch her son's body. She held his cold hand. His arm was loose and heavy. She could see broken teeth but couldn't open his mouth. She asked the undertaker to lift him onto his side so she could better see a series of dark strips on his back – lash marks, she assumed. Ruth thought of her husband and wished he could be here. Eish, it was hard without a man.

*

Early the next morning, Ruth sat in the front row at the funeral service, a black scarf wrapped tightly around her head. Her heart was beating too fast. Samuel's expensive wooden coffin, the lid closed, rested on a metal trolley, so close she felt she could reach out her arm and touch it. The singing started. The Lord is my Shepherd. There were daffodils in the hall.

Ruth knew that at the same time, at the Apostolic church, Simon's service was taking place. It was a shame they couldn't do these things together.

Finally, around noon, the two coffins were brought to the municipal cemetery on the edge of Tumahole, on a sloping patch of open ground facing north across the river.

It was another hot, clear day. An industrial digger had already scraped out two deep holes beside each other – the latest additions to a pattern of narrow graves, stretching into the distance, towards the crescent of hills. Some graves were marked with upturned bottles, a few with small headstones.

The women – Ruth, Naledi, Susan, their sisters, cousins and a dozen or more relatives – took their seats under two large canopies. Further up the slope a satellite truck was parked. The event was being broadcast live on S.A.B.C. and some local politicians – and one or two national figures – were there to attend. Selected dignitaries stepped forwards to comment on the killings and to condemn white racism.

As the prayers and speeches ended, all the men moved forwards as a group, relieved to find employment, to keep busy, taking turns with a handful of shovels. Ruth lost sight of Samuel's brothers, Elias and Lawrence, who were somewhere in the middle of the crowd. She watched as the men scraped at the chalky red earth, then channelled it down, like a stream, on top of the coffins. A few people coughed as a cloud of bitter dust coiled around the mourners and rose with the gusting wind into the sky.

7

TO LIVE AND PERISH

Magistrate Pillay parked early at the police station on Bree Street, walked through the adjoining courtyard and into the side entrance of the courthouse. She'd tried again to persuade her bosses to get someone else to handle this bail application, but had been told no.

Right, she'd thought, then let's do this properly.

Even in her office she could hear the chants outside the courthouse. Two long walls of razor wire had been dragged across the street, and more than a dozen policemen now filled the space between, dressed in riot gear, tear gas canisters hanging off their belts, and with leashed dogs already baring their teeth.

Shoot the Boer! Shoot the farmer!

The cowards are scared.

Shoot! Shoot!

They rob us, these dogs.

Shoot the Boer!

It was just as Pillay had feared.

At the township end of the street, behind the razor wire, Paul and his E.F.F. colleagues were standing beside a larger group of yellow-shirted A.N.C. supporters. They were singing together now, their feet stamping in unison.

Parys is not for blacks. We are not welcome here – we are not treated as human beings, Paul declared.

We are still oppressed, said his friend Gaddafi.

People are going to be killed on a daily basis. Women are going to be raped, said another E.F.F. supporter, a man named Thomas, who had a scar on his chin and a fondness for apocalyptic predictions.

Paul had actually been up in front of Magistrate Pillay himself, a few months earlier. He'd caught his wife in a tavern sitting with another man, and had, he'd conceded, given her three or four slaps. The police had become involved, and soon he was accused of violating a restraining order. He spent ninety-three days in jail before the magistrate ordered him to pay a fine and suggested he find himself a new wife. He thought Magistrate Pillay was just great, but this new case, it was something difficult.

Pillay stepped from her office into the courthouse's cavernous waiting room with its skylights and its benches, and now she could hear another other song, competing with the chants outside.

Firm and steadfast we shall stand,
At Thy will to live and perish,
Oh South Africa, our land.

At the tourist end of Philip Street, a smaller group of sun-weathered white faces stood behind their own line of razor wire, singing the old national anthem. Many of the Afrikaners wore long beards, and military-style khaki shorts and shirts. Most of them weren't even from Parys. Some were holding old Vierkleur flags or homemade posters claiming that white farmers were victims of an orchestrated genocide.

Politics, Pillay thought to herself. Playing the race card. In the end, it's all about votes.

But it could have been far worse. Far uglier. Earlier that morning, more than five hundred whites had attended an impromptu open-air service at the airstrip outside Parys. The Van der Westhuizen's own pastor had addressed the congregation, which included many right-wingers from out of town, with more than a few rifles.

The pastor had urged them not to fuel the flames of hatred and to let the law take its course. Most of the crowd had taken his advice.

*

Ruth managed to slip through the police cordon and into the packed courtroom. She was nearer the front this time and could hear the Indian woman telling the prosecutor that, no, he could not have more time to prepare his arguments for opposing bail. The magistrate had already asked him if he'd be ready by Tuesday and he'd said yes. She could show him the court transcript if he wanted.

The prosecutor had little new to add, and so the magistrate asked the four accused – Boeta van der Westhuizen, Anton Loggenberg and the Cilliers father and son, both named Johan – to stand.

Bail of five thousand rand each.

The row of hunched shoulders in the dock gently subsided.

Ruth left the courthouse shaking her head. The decision did not seem right to her. The police had caught the right men, hadn't they? Otherwise why would the prosecution be so confident?

On the street outside, news that the magistrate had granted bail soon reached both groups of protesters. The singing resumed. Razor wire shrieked as it skidded across tarmac. Police dogs pulled harder at their leashes.

Five thousand rand, Paul said. So the life of a black person is valued at five thousand rand.

*

Rikki van der Westhuizen had brought enough cash with her to cover her husband's bail and she went straight through the courthouse to pay at the counter.

She'd been to visit Boeta, several times, in the cells and it was a real eye-opener.

You wouldn't lock up your dog there, she thought.

It was terrible, not just for your own people, but for anyone.

8

A NICE, GRATEFUL TOWN

A FEW DAYS LATER, six police cars turned off the motorway and rode in convoy over the crater's rim towards Parys. Captain Francois Laux, wearing a white shirt and brown leather jacket, drove the front car – a cramped, cluttered Polo – with one hand on the wheel and, in his mind's eye, a picture of what was about to unfold inside the town's police station.

Later he'd remember it like a scene from a Hollywood police drama, when the big shots from the F.B.I. stroll into some sleepy office, kick a few legs off desks, and declare "We're taking over this case."

Laux had been on the force for just over forty years. He suspected this investigation would be his last. A big, unusual one to finish on. The son of German immigrants, he was a solid figure with a thick, jowly neck, wavy brown hair, and small eyes in a boyish face. He'd been a former goalkeeper on the national police squad.

The convoy passed the airfield and then the old Dutch Reformed Church, where the farmers congregated every Sunday, parking their freshly scrubbed pickups on the lawn outside.

Farm killings were something of a speciality for Laux and the team from the Bloemfontein office of the Hawks – the

Directorate for Priority Crime Investigation. Many of those in the convoy had been working together for twenty years, tearing along the potholed back roads of the Free State, chasing trouble. When Laux shut his eyes, he could flick through old crime scenes like a slide projector.

The meat hook through an old lady's chin, and the long dried bloodstain where she'd been dragged through the house. A thin body wrapped inside an old carpet and stuffed under the bed. A single gunshot to the heart. A grey-haired skull splintered by an axe blow. That woman hidden under the meat in her freezer – not his case, but who could forget it? Torchlight in a dark bedroom and bloody footprints on a white bedspread. Wire from a coat-hanger pushed through wide eyes. A hot iron pressed onto sagging flesh. An electric drill through both kneecaps.

Torture. Always torture.

In all his years on the force – back in the old apartheid days and now – Laux had never arrested a white person for a farm murder. It was always the blacks, always the workers turning on their bosses, or their bosses' neighbours. Statistics explained most of it, and these days that meant that sometimes new black farmers got targeted too. But not so often, he thought. In Parys all fifty-four members of the local farmers' union were still white. In Laux's mind, that fact helped explain the spectacular violence that came with so many of the killings – it wasn't just torturing to get them to open the safe, but something wanton, superfluous, and vengeful. Something racial. Not like the quick, impersonal murders in the towns and townships.

Then again, the frenzy that accompanied the killings tended

to make the Hawks' job easier. There were very few occasions these days when Laux and his men didn't catch the killers – he claimed the police in the Free State had a 97 per cent success rate on farm murders.

"He just goes in, doesn't care about cleaning up the scene, fingerprints, D.N.A., shoe prints. These are not killers who plan the whole thing. It's spur of the moment," Laux would tell schools or community groups in Bloemfontein, pinning up his well-worn crime scene photos on the wall, and waiting for the flood of gory, or anxious, questions.

As Laux walked up the steps and into the police station's gloomy reception, he tried to hold onto the cockiness he'd felt in the convoy. They were the big city team, here to take over from the amateurs. In fact, he knew Parys well. As a child he'd come on holiday here with his parents, and his two sons were studying just up the road at Potchefstroom University. He'd also solved another case here not long ago, a nasty little murder involving a white guy and his two sons who'd killed a local white businessman who owed them money. They'd buried him alive. Everyone had seemed happy with Laux's work. A nice, grateful town.

But this case was going to be very different. From what he'd heard and read so far, and from what his instincts told him, the local police – the white police – were involved in some sort of cover-up.

It had to be. Why else would they have failed to secure the murder scene? It was there in the case notes. Ludicrous. They must be too close to the farming community, too preoccupied by the story of the old white man being attacked, too quick to believe him, and too ready to see the whole thing as a collective beating gone wrong, rather than as the brutal race crime that Laux's bosses had ordered him to investigate. The pressure – from Bloemfontein, and even from Pretoria – was strong. Unusually so. The politicians obviously wanted this one solved quickly and emphatically.

Maybe some of these officers coming forward now and grudgingly shaking hands with the new arrivals were involved in the killings themselves. Laux had read their statements and he had some questions.

We're taking over, on instructions from the National Commissioner. You must give us all the information and documents relating to the case, Laux announced to a silent, sullen room.

This was going to be uncomfortable. And not just with the police. Laux was used to co-operation from white farming communities, but this time he was on the other side from them. They would, without doubt, see him as a traitor. Too bad. It was time to shake the tree and see what fell out.

*

Captain Henk Prinsloo, a tall, slim, middle-aged man in grey glasses, with the easy demeanour of a country doctor, had watched the Hawks arrive. Arrogant, he thought to himself. Looking to scare us all.

Prinsloo had a clear conscience.

The day of the killings had been his first day back on duty after months spent recovering from an accident and subsequent reconstructive surgery on his elbow. He'd just got home from the station when Pieter Kemp, an ex-soldier who ran a volunteer group assisting with rural safety, called him to report that Loedie van der Westhuizen had pressed a panic button. Prinsloo asked him to find out more, went back to the station, picked up a squad car, and headed out to the Weiveld crossroads. On the way, Kemp called him again to say they'd caught the attackers and were planning to take them back to Bulrush, Oom Loedie's farm. They agreed that was a bad idea. They didn't want the scenes cross-contaminating. But then another call came through. It was one of the farmers, sounding nervous. Too many people were arriving now and they were getting aggressive. Out of control. Prinsloo was having trouble finding the location, but he needed to hurry.

He reached the field just before 8.00 p.m. and counted about twenty pickups, some already leaving. He recognised Boeta van der Westhuizen, Oom Loedie's son, and the enormous, unmistakable figure of Anton Loggenberg. Boeta told Prinsloo that the two thieves were in the back of Anton's pickup. He switched on his torch and walked over to take a look.

The two black men were not moving. Their eyes were closed. Prinsloo went back to his car and got a bottle of water to pour on their faces. He could see a few cuts and bruises, but nothing too serious. Simon, on his back, opened his eyes and tried to answer when Prinsloo asked him his name, but he couldn't talk clearly. Samuel's eyes opened too, and started to focus, but he said nothing. Then Simon asked, haltingly, for water to drink and started coughing when Prinsloo leaned into the back of the bakkie and poured some into his mouth. The policeman couldn't lift him up to drink, with his arm still weak after the operation.

There was a crowd of people gathered around the back of the pickup. Besides Boeta and Anton, there was a tall white man Prinsloo didn't recognise, and two black farmworkers.

The police captain's focus was on the farm attack. Where is the gun? Prinsloo asked Simon, leaning over the side of the bakkie and jabbing him with his torch. What were you two doing there?

Simon pointed towards his friend, and said something, maybe about Samuel throwing the gun away. Prinsloo went off to try to get a mobile signal so he could call the dog unit in Sasolburg. Then two colleagues arrived and began the business of transferring the two injured men from the bakkie into their police van.

At this point Prinsloo left the field and drove back to Parys. So much for his first day back at work.

The two blacks had been roughed up, for sure. But nothing that would kill them.

*

The Hawks team decided to set up shop away from the police station, so Captain Laux and his colleagues loaded up all the evidence collected so far and drove it over to a guesthouse across the river, up the slope towards the crater's northern rim, a fancy place called Lavender Hills. A dozen men. No expense spared for this case.

Well, Prinsloo thought, good luck to them. There was always money available when politics got involved.

Prinsloo had been the youngest police lieutenant in the Free State. That was back in the old days. Twenty years ago – 1996 – he'd been promoted to captain. That was his last promotion. He shrugged it off. Policing was a vocation, like being a nurse or a teacher. Some of his white colleagues were less philosophical about their stalled career paths. Jan Le Roux, for instance, was still a warrant officer. He'd been running on the spot for twenty-two years now, watching black officers with far less experience rise through the ranks. It wasn't fair. Sure, apartheid was wrong, but people always twisted it into something even worse. Le Roux's brother had left the force and opened a shop near Pretoria. He was shot dead in 2000. Three bullets to the stomach, one through the neck.

Still, at least the police salary had improved in recent years. And the guys who'd quit to find work in private security companies were now finding it hard going and clamouring, unsuccessfully, to come back onto the force.

In Parys, the remaining white officers knew they just had to knuckle down and remember their pensions.

*

The Hawks' team was divided into three groups, the plan being to spread out and check all the statements the Parys police officers had taken.

Two days after their arrival Laux and his commander,

Colonel Deon Topkin, set out for the farms. Their first call was to the Cilliers family's weather-beaten white house, which stood on a neatly tended lawn. The front door opened and a sheepdog and a puppy muscled their way out, followed by a tall, lithe, pale brown hunting dog, and then by the solid figure of Johan Cilliers Senior. It was his son, also Johan, who had caught Samuel, ordering him to sit down, as he ran across the edge of their property.

Cilliers was polite, but firm.

You can come in, he told Laux. But not your partner.

Topkin was mixed race – Indian, and a little German. He was not as big a man as Laux, and softer spoken, with a contemplative demeanour. He wore a moustache that curled around the corners of his mouth and his black hair was beginning to thin. Some people said Topkin had unreadable eyes, but Laux didn't have to be told what he was thinking at that moment.

Laux sighed, and said that, in that case, they would have to conduct the interviews outside on the lawn.

The conversation didn't go well. Cilliers was angry that he and his son had been arrested. After all, they'd been the ones calling the police from the scene, to tell them to hurry, that the other farmers were getting out of control. But it was also obvious that the general feeling now among all the farmers was that they should all just keep quiet. The coroner would deal with the matter and then they could all get on with life.

Laux and Topkin walked away empty-handed and got back in their car. The road took them in a loop to the north east, across the faded ripples of the crater's edge, and to Loedie van der Westhuizen's big farm with its dark strip of trees, tyres heaped in the long grass, and shabby red-roofed outhouses filled with expensive tractors. As the crow flies, or a dog runs, it was just under four kilometres away from the Cilliers.

Oom Loedie, whose wounds had more or less healed, invited both men inside. He was still living on his own. He still had his three dogs.

Maybe you could put it down to an old man's confusion during a terrifying episode. Maybe the shock had just scrambled everything in his head. But his story about the attack seemed to be changing. He'd seemed calm to the officers who'd interviewed him immediately afterwards, but now he was giving the Hawks a slightly different version, or versions, of what had happened.

The two blacks were standing outside the fence around his home when he got back, not inside it. He might already have been inside the house, not just arriving home. He might have gone outside to confront them. He'd tried to hit the men with a plastic mop. Laux had seen the broken remains of it by the door. Was that how he got the wound on his head? It seemed so.

And the gash on his arm? Topkin asked.

The gash? He'd caught his arm on the door as he'd rushed through the house to press the panic button.

It didn't quite add up. An elderly man, armed with a mop, confronting two young men – gangsters with handkerchiefs over their faces – as they brandished a gun. And where was this gun, anyway?

Oom Loedie had definitely called his son Boeta, whose farm was about seven kilometres further north, on his mobile. At the time, Boeta and his family were lounging round their pool. But what about the panic button? The Hawks had records from the security company in Parys showing that he hadn't hit the panic button until 5.50 p.m. – a whole forty minutes *after* he'd called his son – by which time Boeta had already spread the word on the farmers' WhatsApp group and the hunt was on.

Why had the old man waited so long before pressing the panic button?

Topkin and Laux looked at each other as they walked back to the car. This was not an ordinary farm attack.

*

The Hawks had decided to divide their teams by race, more or less. Black officers to interview black witnesses. A few days later a team called in to say they'd been talking to a black farmworker, Thomas Direko, who was the foreman on one of the biggest, wealthiest and most successful cattle farms in the country – eleven thousand hectares straddling the motorway, eight thousand cattle, a prize-winning maize crop and forty-six workers.

This was the Dannhauser farm, north of Oom Loedie's land.

Kobus Dannhauser had been chairman of the Parys Agricultural Union for the past twenty-fve years. A short, almost comically stocky man with a silver moustache and skin as brown as the surrounding dirt roads, at one time he had been on friendly terms with Nelson Mandela. A hundred and forty years of local family history made the Dannhausers among the very first white farmers to lay claim to the rich soil around Parys. The Van der Westhuizens, by contrast, had only been around for eighty years.

Like quite a few of Dannhauser's workers, Thomas Direko had lived his entire life on the farm, as had his parents before him, and now enjoyed the sort of relationship with his boss that veered – depending on your perspective – between a benevolent paternalism and something more feudal. It was fairly unusual for a black person to be in a position of such responsibility on the farms. Most commercial farmers were white and either hired landless white men as managers – like Fanie Oosthuizen at Weifeld farm – or left it to their sons and, on occasion, daughters.

The Dannhausers were on holiday over Christmas and New Year – not up at their game farm bordering the Kruger National Park but down at their property in Cape Town. They were still away when the WhatsApp message pinged on Dannhauser's phone sometime after 5.00 p.m. on Wednesday, January 6, 2016.

"Can you bring your pickups – Oom Loedie has just been attacked. We're hunting for the people."

He immediately called Direko, who was working in the big yard where the cattle were being fed, right beside the motorway.

You better go along and see what's happening, Dannhauser said.

Direko went to get the pickup and asked another worker, Isaac Xhalisa, to go with him. They set off towards Oom

Loedie's farm, but before they'd even reached the grain silos at the Weiveld crossroads, his boss called again.

It's O.K. now. They've caught the two men. There's no sense in getting involved so head back home.

Sir, can I just go there and see who it is? Direko asked.

It made sense. As foreman, he spent much of his time dealing with security and needed to know who was causing trouble on the farms. Kobus did not allow him to carry a gun, but over the years Direko had made plenty of arrests, catching youngsters from Tumahole stealing fences, or timber, or mealies. Direko had something of a reputation. He would tie suspects' hands with twine and sit on them until the police arrived. If they arrived. Some people said he could be violent.

It's just so I'll recognise them if I see them again on the farm, he told Dannhauser.

O.K.

Thomas turned right at the crossroads and headed south, circling to the west past Bulrush farm, towards the field where the men had been arrested. There was another car directly in front of him. He recognised Captain Prinsloo, the tall officer from Parys.

It was dusk now and getting darker by the minute. The two vehicles pulled off the road and bumped slowly over the rough fields to where they could see activity. They parked and Direko followed the captain on foot to the back of a white pickup, which was surrounded by white farmers. He peered over and immediately recognized Tjixa – Samuel Tjixa – slumped against the cabin. He didn't know the other man.

Both men were in a bad way. Direko noticed that neither man's hands were tied.

Look what the dogs have done to them, Boeta van der Westhuizen said.

Direko looked but he couldn't see any obvious bite marks. He spoke, briefly, to the two Cilliers – father and son – who were also standing nearby, and then he called his boss again.

They have arrested both men. But they're hurt. Hurt bad.

You should leave then, Kobus Dannhauser instructed. I don't want you to get involved.

*

Weeks later, back home and drinking tea with a visitor in his trophy-laden lounge – five leopard skins and the heads of an eland, a buffalo and a lion on the wall, and a stuffed lioness' head lolling beside him on the coffee table – Dannhauser glanced at his phone to see a new WhatsApp message. It was from the E.F.F. in town – a statement from Paul and his colleagues demanding that people boycott any produce from the farms belonging to those implicated in the killings.

"It will be unfair to let the farmers carry on with their lives and to make money using cheap labour. They still view us as monkeys and objects of their target practice," read the text.

Kobus wanted to laugh. It would be the blacks who suffered – who lost their jobs. It was all just so bloody silly.

He nodded his thanks to the uniformed housekeeper as she poured more tea.

"This wasn't a racist incident," Dannhauser explained to his visitor. "If a white guy attacked Mr van der Westhuizen, he'd get the same treatment. I don't say he'd be dead but ... If your relationship with your workers is good, you don't have anything to worry about. But after working hours you don't go to a farm. If the dogs bark at night on my farm I will definitely shoot anyone that is outside my house."

They walked outside, where Thomas Direko was up a ladder, fixing a water tank at the side of the farmhouse. On the lawn below sat two stone cherubs and a clutch of carved rabbits.

Direko had recently been called in by the Hawks to an ID parade. They wanted him to pick out Captain Prinsloo from a line-up, which he'd done. The two men knew each other from way back. In fact, Direko had been a police reservist for a few years but it hadn't worked out.

Now Direko had a story to tell about Prinsloo's actions that night in January. He climbed down the ladder, took a seat near one of the cherubs, and – looking first at his boss for permission – began to talk.

The way Direko remembered it, Prinsloo had been standing towards the back of Anton Loggenberg's white pickup, looking at Samuel's swollen head. He saw Boeta splash some water on the man's face. Then a flashlight swung towards the other injured man, the one lying flat across the darkened well of the vehicle. Direko watched Captain Prinsloo pull out a short black rod, maybe fifteen centimetres long, and jab it towards the man's underpants, prodding him in his private parts.

Tell me – what were you two doing out here? Prinsloo asked the man.

Direko recognised the rod. They used something similar on the farm to manage the cattle. To shock them.

9

SUICIDE RISK

A T LAST THE weather changed. Rain, then an early autumn cold front rushing in from the south. A thick funnel of mist coated the Vaal River at dawn, as if a steam train had just rumbled through. To the east, in the refinery town of Sasolburg, Ruth Qokotha sniffed at the familiar, acrid air, and pushed her hands deeper into the pockets of her beige anorak.

I'm not fat, she said to her neighbour. It's just all these clothes to make me warm. They laughed. Ruth was never short of something to say. Perhaps it was her mother's doing, for giving her the middle name Hletjiwe – the one they gossip about.

She took a minibus taxi to the town centre, walked into the Department of Labour, and joined the queue. There was a young white lady in front of her, with strips of purple in her hair, and a prominent black eye. Seeing this made Ruth think about her husband, Elias, who had tried to beat her, once or twice, towards the end, when he was drinking. The thought almost made her smile – eish! He would try – but she would kick him back harder.

Ruth was struggling with the administration required to claim unemployment benefit. Her bank account had been closed a while back, and she didn't understand the forms they kept giving her. She would sometimes show them to strangers, asking them to explain what the numbers meant – what were the insurance contributions that Hector had been paying at the farm, and what was the money she could now expect to receive. When she got to the front of the queue, the official said Ruth needed to be patient, that the paperwork was still being processed, and that she really did need to open a new account. He gave her another form.

The logistics of leaving La Rochelle farm had not been easy. The A.N.C. had helped out one last time, paying for transport to ferry her possessions to the shack she'd begun building a few years earlier, in the township of Zamdela, just outside Sasolburg. But she could only fit one bed, a mattress, a cupboard and a few other things in the van. She'd had to leave the fridge, a dressing table, and two big mattresses on the farm. She'd also had to leave her chickens. And now she was completely broke, borrowing money from relatives and neighbours for food, and also looking after the boys, Elias and Lawrence, who stayed with her in Zamdela but had no incomes either.

They were right on the edge of the township, backing onto a field of stubble, and the recent rains had flooded the path from the main road. Their shack was not much bigger than Naledi's place in Tumahole. Corrugated-iron sheets on a wooden frame, a dirt floor partly covered in a strip of orange linoleum, the double bed to the left of the doorway, and the kitchen area to the right. No windows, no electricity, no toilet, a communal tap outside beside a patch of dirt that Ruth swept clean every morning, and a puppy called Romeo who slept by the door at night. Ruth had decided to let her sons sleep on the double bed. She slept on coats and a blanket spread over the linoleum.

There was a policeman, Tshabalala, who sometimes got in touch with Ruth. He was from Sasolburg and had been the original investigating officer on Samuel's case, before the Hawks team had stepped in. Ruth once asked him if he could take her to the field where her son had died, so she could try to find his spirit, but Tshabalala had said no, that he'd died in hospital, that he'd seen Samuel there that night and had tried to speak to him. Samuel had opened his mouth but nothing came out.

Ruth didn't think it was worth going to the hospital. Too many dead. Too many spirits.

Now Tshabalala kept her informed about the next court dates, and sometimes gave her a lift into Parys.

One morning he told her that someone else had been arrested.

A fifth man. A policeman.

*

Captain Prinsloo stood in his bedroom trying hard not to lose his temper, not to lash out at the Hawks officers who had driven up to his house in their big convoy. His wife, Rona, was crying; so were their two teenaged daughters, Arne and Alicia. His mother was in the kitchen. It was outrageous.

Can we just have a minute? Prinsloo asked the officer again. Two of them had followed him into his bedroom when he went to pack and get changed out of his uniform.

You want to see me naked? Is that it? He was still trying to keep things light. That was his usual way.

No, you're a suicide risk, they told him. He would not be allowed to wear a belt, or shoelaces.

Rona and the girls came into the bedroom, still in tears, and Prinsloo asked the officers, again, if they'd please leave.

I need a minute to pray with my family, to calm them down. No.

So Prinsloo kneeled on the floor, with his wife and girls beside him. They held hands. Dear God, please be with my family and keep them safe.

One of the officers began to cry and left the room. The other stayed. When the prayers were over, as Prinsloo was walking out of the bedroom, he told him, I hope something like this will never happen to you.

The arrest itself was not a complete surprise. Prinsloo had been asked to attend an identity parade and he knew Thomas Direko would have picked him out as the officer he'd seen by the pickup that night. Something was up. Immediately afterwards, Prinsloo had been to see Captain Laux – officer to officer – and had assured him that, if there was to be an arrest, he would come to the station voluntarily, or appear in court. He was hardly going to make a run for it.

Instead, the Hawks turned up at his home, at 5.00 p.m., too late in the day to post bail, guaranteeing him a night in jail. Although Laux insisted the timing was a coincidence, and they were just playing it straight, Prinsloo was sure it was deliberate.

They didn't handcuff him. The police took him back to the station, searched his office, his car, looking for the cattle prod, or Taser, then confiscated his mobile to see if he had any footage from the scene. He didn't. Then they began questioning him, challenging the statement he'd written the day after the attacks.

The whole Hawks team was in the room, hammering away at him for an hour and a half. And not just about the recent killings. They knew about the man who'd died after climbing an electricity pole a while back on Boeta van der Westhuizen's farm.

Were you with him? Were you there when Boeta electrocuted the kaffir?

Kaffir. Kaffir. They were throwing the word at him, trying to rile him, seeing that it was working.

Colonel Topkin, I don't use that language, Prinsloo said, trying to appeal to the man in charge.

Why do you want to protect the farmers?

Why won't you tell us what happened?

Who killed those kaffirs?

The questions kept coming. Eventually they got to the Taser.

Prinsloo was staggered. Not just because it was all nonsense. But because of the way he was being treated by his fellow officers. He knew the Hawks were under pressure, maybe even big political pressure, but still. As he was leaving the room, he recalled, Laux delivered a final taunt.

You will be in jail, and your wife and children on the streets, homeless, by the time I've finished with you.

10

TELL NOBODY

THE COUSINS WERE looking for somewhere private. Somewhere discreet. They decided on a neighbour's mealie field, which was off the main dirt road to Parys. They swung through the gate and kept going, eighteen-year-old Loedie in front, driving his father's red pickup. When they'd gone far enough, when they knew the cars could not be seen, they stopped and got out. Loedie reached into the back of the pickup to grab the can of petrol and a fan-belt. Muller took charge of the shoes. Then they all set off, striding deeper into the field of dry mealies like kids on an adventure, looking for a patch of open ground where they could light the fire, far from prying eyes.

They felt furtive, maybe even scared. But mostly they were anxious to put the lives they'd always planned – lives that had stretched ahead of them so clearly, so confidently, for so many years – back on track.

Loedie was the only son of accused number 1, Boeta van der Westhuizen. He was scrumhalf-small, with a jumpy swagger, a mop of blond hair, his father's long nose, and (having dropped out of school) no plans beyond working on the family's beef and maize farm. His cousin Muller van der Westhuizen was a year older and a foot taller. He had short curly hair, a round, doughy face, and the confident air of a prefect – explained perhaps by the fact that his father, Vicky van der Westhuizen, was widely considered to be the most successful farmer of his generation in the extended family.

Loedie, Muller, Wian, Wicus, Cor Loggenberg, Harvey Coetzee from a neighbouring farm – they'd all grown up together, racing their fathers' cars and tractors, hunting, braaiing, comfortably in and out of each other's kitchens, and when they got older, tearing into Parys on the weekends to play rugby, to watch the match at A.B.'s bar, meet girls at the Cherry on Top, drink Fokof lager on tap at the Pickled Pig, and maybe end a big night down on the dance floor at Legends before driving blearily back home. Some of the cousins spoke good Sesotho or isiXhosa, but their close friends were white, and their classes were mostly segregated by language, which meant the races were still nudged apart. Most of the farmers in the district put their boys in Parys High School; if they could manage the fees they might send them to boarding school in Potchefstroom.

Every Wednesday evening, some of the older cousins would gather at Loedie's older sister's place. Crista was engaged to Gert Janse van Rensburg, known to everyone as Miela, a big, cheerful man who fixed tractors at a garage in Sasolburg. The two of them had recently moved into a spare cottage on a nearby farm. Crista worried that the cousins didn't eat properly. No vegetables. Shame. So she'd cook something decent for them, and they'd all sit together watching the sun set, talking about sport, and farming, and crime, and making plans for next year. It had become a tradition.

Except that now everything was getting complicated.

A few weeks after the deaths, the Van der Westhuizen clan

had been summoned to a meeting in town. Boeta had been granted bail, but now that the Hawks were causing trouble, the farmers' early sense of impunity had begun to transform into something much warier. And so they'd gone as a group to see a family friend and lawyer, Kobus Burger, who'd arranged for them to gather at his father-in-law's home in Parys.

As Muller recalled it, they'd sat outside, on garden chairs, to discuss the case and what needed to be done. Everyone knew about the photos. There were rumours about a video circulating too, showing the two black thieves either being beaten, or lying in the back of the pickup. It was hardly surprising really. Everyone filmed everything nowadays.

Burger had a strict warning for them all.

You must clear everything off your phones, he instructed. Make sure there is nothing on them that could incriminate you. And you must say nothing. If you say nothing – nothing will happen.

Muller quickly deleted two photos from his mobile and hoped that the lawyer was right. Maybe this really would blow over.

At least that was Muller's version. Burger would later insist, forcefully, that it was nonsense – part of a shabby conspiracy to discredit him. But as Muller claimed to remember it, the lawyer had that way of talking, confident, bullish, always on the attack. Before long Burger was telling them that they could sue the police for the way they'd been treated, that they'd win so much money that each of them would be able to go out and buy themselves a brand new 4 × 4. Just pick the colour. Easy.

*

Some of the Van der Westhuizens were not so sure.

Neils van der Westhuizen, Wicus' father, was one.

Away on an overseas trip, he called his son. This is serious – much more serious than any of you think. Do you hear me? He wanted his boy to lie low – maybe even leave the country. They had relatives farming in Mozambique.

You must get away, he said. Get to your mom's and tell nobody. Wicus' parents were divorced.

But, Pa, is it not going to look like I'm running away? Wicus asked.

Just say to everyone that you have to fetch stuff for me. Make sure you get to your mom's this weekend. Do you hear me? You get in your truck and—

—you tell nobody! That was his stepmother, panicking, shouting in the background.

You say nothing. You know nothing. If someone asks you, you know nothing. I will think of a plan. Just do what I say, Neils said.

*

There were more meetings.

Vicky van der Westhuizen invited the farmers to his home in Parys. They were unanimous. Everyone must stand together.

Boeta called a meeting with a smaller group, the younger farmers, at Cook's Rest.

Anton Loggenberg, Boeta's oldest friend, attended that meeting. Anton wasn't a member of the local farmers' union, which met on the first Tuesday of the month – harvest permitting – at a small building close to Boeta and Rikki's thatched house, to socialise and talk business and, sometimes, to pray for rain. He maintained that he had no need for the union. He spoke isiXhosa and got on fine with the blacks. He also didn't need to be on the farmers' WhatsApp security group. Some of his neighbours saw these things in a different light. Anton was a troublemaker, an outlier, not be trusted. He had stolen cattle in the past, they claimed, and reneged on deals. All lies, Anton insisted.

Now Boeta and Anton stood in front of the young farmers and tried to put the fear of God into them. At least that was how it struck Muller, and some of the others. The two older men talked about their time in jail, about how neither of them had given the Hawks anything, hadn't told them who was at the scene that night, hadn't pointed fingers at anyone. And that was the way it had to remain. Kobus Burger was right. Say nothing, and nothing will happen.

Then came the threat. Muller recalled that it was made by both Oom Boeta and Oom Anton, and that it was not subtle, not a quiet hint, but rather something designed to intimidate and to silence.

If anyone talks, we'll cut out their tongues.

*

Muller had already burned his shirt at home. He'd got blood all down his shoulder when he'd helped to carry one of the blacks and put him in the back of Anton's pickup. He'd been so worried about it that after he left the scene he drove straight back to Weiveld farm and changed into a fresh shirt. The business with the shoes came later – Boeta's idea, according to Muller.

Boeta had asked Loedie to call the cousins – anyone who'd kicked the suspects – and tell them to come immediately to Cook's Rest. And to bring with them the shoes they'd worn that night.

Muller got the call and he drove over. The sitting room was in darkness when he arrived but then Boeta came through from his bedroom. He told the cousins to gather all the shoes, then find somewhere quiet and burn them. And not to tell anyone, of course. When Muller pointed out that he'd not done any kicking, Boeta had said, Too bad, there might be blood on his shoes anyway, or maybe he'd left footprints at the scene. They couldn't take chances now that the Hawks were sniffing around.

On the road, driving towards Parys, they ran into their cousin Wicus. He was still wearing the same shoes he'd worn that night. They told him to take them off there and then and put them in the back with the others. Then they drove on, through the gate, and into the mealie field. When they found a cleared patch they piled the shoes together in a heap. Loedie added the fan-belt and then sprinkled everything with petrol. Loedie's boots had steel toecaps. Muller recalled how they'd wondered if they'd burn.

And that was it. They'd cleaned their mobile phones. They'd burned the evidence. They would stick together.

And it wasn't because they were trying to fool the police or get away with murder. It was just to protect themselves from a rotten system that was trying – was always trying – to scapegoat the white farmers.

It was just like their lawyer, Kobus Burger, had said.

"These Hawks are crooks, man. Bloody crooks."

11

A MURDERER'S CHILD

SEVEN MEN STOOD in the dock in Magistrate Pillay's courtroom.

It was a Monday afternoon in March 2017, and the protests outside the court had finally subsided.

It's all bullshit, Kobus Burger muttered, his face half turned towards his clients.

The Hawks had been busy. They had statements from more than a dozen black farmworkers.

The four original accused – Boeta van der Westhuizen, Anton Loggenberg, and the Cilliers father and son – who had since been joined by Captain Henk Prinsloo, were all there.

But now there were two new faces in the dock and the mood in the courtroom was changing. More confrontational. Sharp glances and snide comments.

Laux and Topkin were in their usual places, seated near the door with three other Hawks officers. In front of them sat the prosecution team. Alongside the original advocate, the one who'd angered Pillay in January, sat another figure, an unexpectedly senior one. J.J. Mlotshwa was a deputy director in the National Prosecuting Authority, sent to Parys from Pretoria.

For a simple bail hearing. It was unheard of. The clearest sign yet that this case was now being watched closely at the highest levels.

Pillay had her own problems. She knew what was coming. Her boss had called earlier to warn her. The A.N.C. Youth League had been complaining about her. So had other people in the party. She needed to watch her step.

Sure enough, after a tetchy exchange about how late the court might be sitting today, the junior prosecutor suddenly announced that the state wanted Pillay to recuse herself. He said she'd been spotted at the weekend talking to Captain Prinsloo and his family in the supermarket in Parys.

"Yes, I met and greeted them … as is my constitutional right," Pillay snorted. "This court has nothing to hide."

"You will never be impartial," the prosecutor shot back.

"You are insulting this court," Pillay said.

She shook her head angrily and tore off the sheet of paper on which she'd been taking notes as if it were soiled. She was not going to back down or take any more nonsense. This isn't Zimbabwe, she told herself.

*

In the dock, an unshaven Boeta van der Westhuizen looked gloomy. He had good reason. He had messed up. His temper had got the better of him again.

A few days earlier, sitting at a restaurant on Bree Street, he had decided to call Captain Laux. He didn't like the way the Hawks were treating him, his family, his workers, the whole case and he told him so.

Two days before that, Laux and his team had driven to the Mbeki neighbourhood of Tumahole to pick up a black farmworker called Phineas Rasenyalo and take him to the Hawks' guesthouse for questioning. According to Rasenyalo – who made a formal complaint in a signed affidavit soon after the incident – Laux had shouted at him, demanding that he sign a statement implicating the white farmers, telling him that the whites were lying, that the whites were "going to kill me if I tell the truth". Then Laux "punched me on my left eye and on my head and he kicked me on my behind". Another black farmworker was brought into the same room. He later confirmed that the Hawks had threatened him too. He said they had assaulted Rasenyalo in front of him. Laux denied this – just as he denied Prinsloo's claims of threats and intimidation.

From the restaurant on Bree Street, Boeta dialled Laux's number. The Hawks team were sitting at the guesthouse, and Laux switched on the speakerphone so the others could hear Boeta's rant.

If you ever come near my farm again, if you try to intimidate my workers again, I'm going to fuck you up. I'll punch a hole in your head.

The Hawks turned up at Cook's Rest at seven the next morning. They came with an armed response unit. They went in heavy, dragging Boeta away from his breakfast and bundling him into a van. Boeta found himself back in jail, perhaps until the case came to trial. That would teach him.

Now, in addition to everything else, accused number 1 was facing charges of intimidation and of violating his bail conditions. Beside him in the dock, accused number 2, Anton

Loggenberg, was sitting on a cushion, his stomach drooping between his legs, hands clasping his knees. He was a handsome man, with a strong jaw and thick greying hair, but, as his wife Gusta explained, "when he's stressed, he eats." Anton and Boeta were distant cousins and had been friends since schooldays in Parys. Boeta had been best man at Anton's wedding. People often bracketed them together, Anton and Boeta. A couple of characters with a reputation as local scoundrels and lousy farmers, always making excuses, and always drinking and fighting. They had told the police the same story about that night, the night of the incident. They had both arrived at the scene after it was all over, after the two blacks had already been beaten up. And that was all they planned to say on the matter. The Hawks could fuck off. Anton and Boeta had also both said that too – to their faces.

I'm going to fucking sue you, Captain Laux remembered Anton shouting at him, banging on the side of his vehicle, accusing him of harassing his farmworkers. Then Anton had tried to get him to come into his house, alone, for a chat. No chance. Laux wasn't going to fall for that.

Anton still wanted the Hawks to look for the gun, the one the blacks had used to assault Oom Loedie. He was convinced they'd find it in the mud at the bottom of one of Oom Loedie's two big water tanks. He'd told Laux. He'd called Laux and told him he would drain those two tanks himself and pay for the expense. Then – when they found the gun – *then* they'd understand why the farmers had roughed those two up. But Anton's lawyer had warned him against taking this action, saying that if the Hawks found a gun there they would be sure to accuse him of planting it, and would use it against him in court.

It was obvious to Anton that the Hawks weren't interested in investigating the farm attack. It was typical. They only got excited when it was a white attacking a black, never the other way around.

Later, Laux would swear that his team had, in fact, drained the damned tanks and had found nothing. No gun.

*

Anton was still out on bail. He was just in court today because those were the rules. The same went for the two Cilliers. Actually, the Hawks had told the Cilliers they were in the clear – that nobody had said a word against the father and son. Maybe now would be a good time for them to explain what had really happened, but they were staying quiet.

Captain Prinsloo had also been granted bail. Now here he was, standing in the dock, in the middle of the farmers. A solitary figure in his jacket and tie, trying, and failing, to keep his distance from the other accused. At least the town had rallied behind him, raising money to help with his legal fees, organising a golf day, that sort of thing. He was due to pay off the mortgage on his house in two months, but now that wasn't looking likely.

At the far end of the dock, the two newest accused – accused numbers 6 and 7 – looked tired and fidgety.

Young Wian van der Westhuizen's ankle had healed since January, when he'd boasted to anyone who would listen that he'd injured it kicking the two black thieves. Beside him stood another white man from the farming community – Fanie Oosthuizen, the foreman at Weiveld farm, who'd joked about one of the attackers looking like a train had run over him and had shared the photo on his mobile.

Fanie had once been a prison warder, then he'd gone down the gold mines – five kilometres down, hot, sweltering – installing timber supports in the new shafts. Then, eighteen years ago, he and his wife, Joelene, had decided to settle on the farms and since then both of them had worked for Vicky van der Westhuizen on Weiveld. Fanie was an easy-going man, a joker who accepted his place in the farm hierarchy. He knew that the Van der Westhuizen boys looked down on him; after all, he didn't own land. He was just a worker, like the blacks. A different class to the white land owners' sons.

The Hawks had leaned hard on Fanie over the last few days. He'd told his lawyer, Jan Ellis, that Topkin and Laux had threatened him, telling him they'd lock up his son and his brother, that they knew all three of them had been at the scene that night. They could be charged with "common purpose" and spend twenty years in prison, even if they hadn't lifted a finger themselves against the blacks.

If you don't co-operate, then it will be war, Laux said.

Please, I'm talking to you as a father and a human being, Fanie had pleaded.

If you don't talk, your son is going to jail, Topkin replied.

On the other hand, the Hawks told Fanie, if he decided to talk, and if he were to consider becoming a witness for the prosecution ...

In that case, the Hawks insisted they would protect Fanie and his family. They told him they understood he might be in danger from some of the other farmers. They were ready to move him and his family away from the area, to put them in a witness protection scheme, somewhere nice, maybe by a river – We know you like fishing – and he'd keep the same salary. And if he wanted to tell a few white lies about his brother and his son's role in those two blacks being assaulted, well, that would be fine too. Fanie had told his lawyer exactly what the Hawks had said to him.

In court, the grey-haired Ellis was fuming. "This is scandalous and vexatious," he declared. The state was abusive and intimidating. And now Captain Laux, over there by door, was chuckling with the other Hawks. "I see the investigating officer is laughing. Is this South Africa? Is this our legal system?" Ellis asked.

Magistrate Pillay appeared to share his frustration. The prosecution still hadn't produced any reasonable grounds for refusing bail. And she was preoccupied with her own battle, conscious of how much court time had been wasted by the demand for her recusal. Now it was too late in the day to finish the bail proceedings for accused numbers 6 and 7. Fanie and Wian were returned to the communal cells behind the courthouse, alongside Boeta.

The farmers' families spilled out into the sunlight.

"We're not happy with the way the Hawks are handling things," Boeta's wife, Rikki, told a reporter. "We don't trust them. And we don't understand the magistrate issue. It's a very emotional situation."

Fanie's boss, the short, bullish Vicky van der Westhuizen, was angrier and more explicit.

"It's a racist plot," he said.

And to prove it, you could look at the sworn affidavits and medical reports from their black farmworkers. These showed that, far from being on the side of the workers, the Hawks had been threatening and had even assaulted them. They had forced them to give false statements incriminating their white bosses.

Defence lawyer Kobus Burger nodded his head vigorously.

"The state is busy with monkey business," he said. "And I have proof."

*

It was a Sunday morning and, with Boeta now in jail, Rikki and her youngest daughter, Marie, had been to church in Parys on their own. Afterwards, Marie was quiet in the car as they turned left at the grain silos and headed back up to the farmhouse. When they got home she went to her parents' bedroom and sat on the bed, thinking about everything. Then she went into the kitchen to get a glass of water.

"Are you O.K.?" Rikki asked.

"I'm fine," Marie told her. "I just need to be left alone for a while."

She took her water, went into her bedroom and closed the door. She sat and thought about what had happened at church, and afterwards, at Sunday School.

Why are you even here?

People, even adults, had said it to her face.

Your father is a killer, so how can you pray to God if your father is going to hell?

Murderer's child. Murderer's child.

It felt like everyone she knew had turned against her, even close friends, children she'd known since nursery school. And now her father was back in jail, her beloved grandfather had been sick ever since the attack, and her mother was dealing with her own stress.

Surely, Marie thought, it would be better for everyone if she was gone. Out of the way.

She swallowed the pills she'd taken from the drawer in her father's bedside cabinet and lay down on her bed.

12

BACKSTABBERS

A FEW DAYS later, Magistrate Pillay slipped into her own courtroom through the public entrance, trying to look nonchalant but feeling like a trespasser as she sought to find a seat near the back.

"This was a brutal and diabolical murder."

It was a grey morning in Parys. At the front of the room the prosecutor was in full flow, arguing against bail for Fanie and Wian, accused numbers 6 and 7.

"A sense of shock and outrage ... the deceased were severely tortured ..."

Pillay sat and listened for a minute or two as the defence lawyers pushed back, arguing that the state had no evidence linking the accused to the killings: there had been "forty farmers ... with cars coming and going" that night. And the Hawks hadn't let up. They had continued to intimidate Fanie and Wian. It was an abuse of process.

Pillay stood up and walked back to the exit, turning to make a small bow towards the man who had just taken over her duties in this case.

It had all happened so fast, she was still reeling, still furious. She knew the political pressure against her had been building. Someone senior in the provincial A.N.C. had called to tell her "the big shots are watching you", and "watch your step". Her name was apparently coming up at local A.N.C. branch meetings. The party's youth league had begun making more formal complaints about her – that she was biased, that her boyfriend was white, that she was a racist for giving the white farmers bail.

Her boss – the man now presiding over the case in her courtroom – had telephoned and asked her to recuse herself because of complaints from the A.N.C.

Pillay had been scornful.

I'm too white? Sometimes I'm too black. Is it the foundation I use?

She would not be pushed out. In fact, she decided she would wear a sari to court the next day just to remind them who she was.

But it was too late. The Hawks had found her weak point.

Over the years Pillay had developed a habit of discussing her work in private with a male friend – in fact, it was the same man who'd sent her the bunch of flowers that had contributed towards her divorce. Bobby Hartslieff was much older than Pillay. He was a well-known Free State businessman, a man with powerful friends and a colourful past. He was also a member of the A.N.C. He and Pillay seemed to have a special connection. Pillay couldn't explain it. She wondered if perhaps they'd known each other in a previous life, it was that intense.

One afternoon they'd talked about the two farm killings and the bail applications over the phone. She told him that the Hawks were useless, that their case was all hearsay, that there was insufficient evidence. No grounds to oppose bail. Hartslieff agreed. He said the Hawks were a bunch of idiots, that in fact he'd been talking to Captain Laux earlier, asking him about bail, and it felt like he understood the rules better than the police did. On the call Hartslieff called her "Magistrate", which seemed unusual.

The next morning the prosecutors asked to speak to her in her chambers. The defence team came too.

We have a recording, the prosecutors said. Of you, with an unknown person.

For weeks now the Hawks and the prosecutors had been losing patience with Magistrate Pillay. Playing it by the book was one thing, but she really did seem to be taking the farmers' side in this case, Laux for one was sure of it. She kept pressuring the state to speed up its investigation, threatening to withdraw the case if they couldn't produce substantial evidence. He thought she wanted it to go as far as an inquest and leave it there.

It was, Pillay later reflected, such an obvious trap. That call out of the blue. Hartslieff must have been sitting with the Hawks team when he'd telephoned her. They had been feeding him questions to ask. Perhaps Hartslieff had even put her on speakerphone so they could hear the whole thing. Now she understood why he'd called her "Magistrate"; it was for the policemen's benefit.

Laux denied this – he said they'd simply worked it out.

Pillay told the lawyers, now seated before her desk, that the unknown person could only be Hartslieff – he was the only person she'd talked to about the case. And in private. Furious with him, with the Hawks, with the whole nonsense, and keen to show that she was the victim of political games, she also pointed out that Hartslieff was a long-standing member of the A.N.C.

Go ahead, she told them all, investigate me. I've got nothing to hide.

And she might have been able to stand her ground. But then the defence lawyers spoke up. This business with the A.N.C. was not helpful. Perhaps it would be better if Pillay recused herself after all.

What the fuck did you do now? she screamed down the phone at Hartslieff later that day. You ruined my life. She wanted to kill him. He insisted that he hadn't put her on speakerphone, that he hadn't betrayed her. He had just been trying to be a good citizen.

*

Two stern-faced women, in bright yellow A.N.C. T-shirts with "Hands off Zuma" on the front, sat just behind the dock as the new magistrate, Ronnie Mguni, glared towards the back of the court through a pair of small, round spectacles. Someone's mobile had just interrupted proceedings.

"So help me God."

On the stand, Colonel Topkin was being sworn in. The Hawks boss rejected the claim that his team had tried to intimidate the accused. As for the suggestion that they'd been beating up farmworkers to secure statements against some of the accused – the truth was the exact opposite. The Hawks now had more than fifteen statements from workers explaining how they'd been taken, in a big group, to Vicky van der

Westhuizen's home on a golf estate in town, to be told by their boss: "I don't want backstabbers on my farm." Mr Van der Westhuizen wanted to know if any of his workers had been threatened or assaulted by the police, or offered money for information. Topkin said that in their statements the workers said that Mr Vicky van der Westhuizen had offered two thousand rand to any worker who could point out someone who'd talked to the police.

"So definitely, they're afraid," Topkin said of the black workers. It was proof that the white farmers were involved in a big cover-up, intimidating their workers into silence. And these two accused here, foreman Fanie Oosthuizen and Wian van der Westhuizen – who both worked for Vicky van der Westhuizen – were part of that.

So, no, they shouldn't get bail.

The two defence lawyers, Kobus Burger and Jan Ellis, began whispering to each other.

The magistrate took his glasses off, leaned forwards, and asked Ellis if he would tell his "friend" to show the court "some respect".

"He's my colleague, not my friend." Ellis bristled at what struck him as a racially loaded remark.

"Friend!" one of the A.N.C. women snorted in derision.

There was a clap of thunder outside, and the promise of rain. The magistrate remarked that Wicus van der Westhuizen was still "at large", and "not yet arrested". A few minutes later, he pointedly corrected Mr Ellis' pronunciation of a farmworker's surname. Perhaps things had changed now that Magistrate Pillay was no longer in charge.

Except the facts had not changed. The Hawks were still offering second-hand testimony, no decent eyewitnesses, no prima facie evidence, no white farmers breaking ranks. The evidence against Fanie and Wian was flimsy too.

Bail was granted, and the new magistrate wondered, out loud, whether this case would ever be completed. Perhaps, he said, it would remain a mystery.

13

TWO DOGS ON A HARE

SOMEONE CALLED Captain Laux with an odd sort of tip-off. Go to the carwash in Parys.

The Executive Car Wash on Water Street was a shabby sort of place, tucked up an alley behind A.B.'s bar, and staffed by half a dozen young black women who waited, with buckets and cloths, for the next farmer to swing off the main road into town from the motorway with a muddy bakkie and, more often than not, a few minutes spare to grab a beer next door.

The girls were lazy, the manager complained. No initiative. You had to watch them all the time. Of course she remembered the strange man with the cowboy hat, brandishing the photos on his mobile of those two blacks, and that offhand, almost sleazy boast – we killed two kaffirs last night.

Laux asked to look at the register for the morning of January 7, 2016 and found two number plates. One of them was familiar. It belonged to Anton Loggenberg, accused number 2. Laux traced the second number to an address in Bothaville, another farming town about an hour's drive out of Parys to the south-west. He got in his car.

The man who answered the door was tall. He had a firm chin, large ears, short grey hair and weathered skin. He leaned on a walking stick, while a fox terrier (called Baba Ganoush, as he told Laux) lurked at his heels.

Ockert van Zyl. Not your usual farmer, Laux thought.

The Hawks captain introduced himself. He outlined what he'd heard at the carwash. He told Van Zyl he was there to arrest him, on suspicion of murder.

Van Zyl listened and then he said, Come in, sit down, have a coffee. Let's talk about this.

*

The farm Van Zyl owned outside Parys lay just beyond the motorway and a fair distance south of the Weiveld crossroads. He didn't spend much time there – it wasn't really his scene, all those farmers, all related to each other, one massive family, all pretending nothing had changed in decades. For him the cattle were more of an investment, a hobby for a loner who'd made his money from scratch in the perfume packaging business. But he was good friends with Anton Loggenberg, even though he knew him as a rascal. The two men had come to a gentlemen's agreement to combine their herds of Brahman cattle and share the workload. In fact they'd just spent the day together on January 6 last year with the big white beasts and Van Zyl was resting back home on his couch, at around half past six, when a neighbour called to tell him there had been a farm attack.

Van Zyl immediately called Loggenberg, who was driving home with his son, Cor, an athletic eighteen-year-old with his father's strong chin, who was home from boarding school for the holidays.

It took Van Zyl a while to find the place. His friend had asked him to bring some diesel for him – his car was running low. And then he got lost trying to find a way through the maze of fencing on the edge of Oom Loedie's property. At one point he'd even had to cut his way through some wire. Hell of a thing to get there.

By the time he got to the field it was dark. Van Zyl didn't recognise many of the shapes moving past him, faces caught in headlights as the crowd of farmers thinned out. But then he spotted Anton's bulky silhouette coming towards him.

Weeks later, when he tried to describe the scene – the atmosphere – at the back of the white pickup, to Captain Laux, having coffee with him in his lounge, Van Zyl experimented with various different expressions. It was no tea party, he offered. It was fast and furious. But the English words felt flat. Then he thought of an Afrikaans phrase, something that captured the savagery, the raw fury of that moment.

It was like two dogs on a hare.

As he approached the vehicle, Van Zyl's first thought was that a black man was dead. He could see someone in a blue sweater slumped, motionless, against the driver's cab. Then he heard a noise.

Tssch!

A loud snap, almost like a gunshot.

Van Zyl peered into the dark well of the bakkie and saw another black man, lying on his back, his jeans pulled down to expose a pair of green underpants. And now he could see what was making that snapping noise.

Van Zyl didn't know Boeta van der Westhuizen well – Anton

had introduced them once, but that was about all. Now he watched Boeta leaning over the black man and whipping his face, hard, with a doubled-up fan-belt. There was light – maybe torchlight – shining on the scene, and Van Zyl could see blood on the man's face, small bubbles in the blood catching the light, and every time the man was hit by the belt the blood sprayed into the air, prompting Van Zyl to step back.

Dogs on a hare.

Where's the gun? Boeta kept asking the man. But Van Zyl couldn't hear a reply.

Then Boeta pointed towards the man's groin. He's wearing my underpants, he said. And my shoes. He must have stolen them.

There was another white man standing beside them in the dark. He was wearing a police uniform. Van Zyl saw him pull out a cattle-prod. He knew the type well – the size of a torch with two points at one end.

Is it working? he heard Boeta ask the officer.

I'll test it on you, the officer had replied, and he'd made a show of jabbing it towards Boeta's arm.

Fuck! I'll fucking beat you, Boeta shouted – half nervous, half laughing.

The policeman had the cattle-prod in one hand and a bottle of water in the other. Then Van Zyl saw him reach into the back of the bakkie and squeeze some water into the man's mouth as if to wake him up. He asked him where the gun was, and then, without warning, he jabbed the electric prodder into the man's green underpants.

*

Ockert van Zyl already knew what the other farmers called him behind his back. Kaffirboetie. He didn't mind. Maybe it was a badge of honour. He'd never gone in for the whole community thing, or marriage for that matter, and he didn't want kids after the childhood he'd endured – kicked off the family farm by a violent father, a bad one, at the age of fourteen. He'd made his own way ever since, lying about his qualifications, eventually heading to Europe to study the perfume business. He was still a loner, an outsider, with his pipe and his black cowboy hat.

It didn't take long for people to hear that Van Zyl was talking to the Hawks, that he'd broken ranks, that he'd dropped Boeta in it, and Captain Prinsloo too.

The threats started soon afterwards, he told Laux. Never direct, never specific, just people passing on things they'd heard. He stopped sleeping at his farm and retreated to Bothaville.

Laux wasn't sure what to make of him. Van Zyl shared his contempt for the idea that there had been a farm attack in the first place at old man Loedie's house.

Ah, man! Come on! Van Zyl would become exasperated by anyone still peddling that theory. "There was no farm attack. Are you telling me that two tough blacks with a gun can't overcome that 73-year-old man? Please!"

But Van Zyl wasn't the ideal witness for the Hawks. He'd only arrived at the scene when things were winding up and had only stayed for a few minutes. More importantly, it was hard to know if and when he was telling the truth. He struck Laux as a maverick, maybe even a bit of a fantasist – not someone to build a case around. And he was obviously protecting his friend Anton, insisting he'd not seen him do anything wrong, even though he'd sometimes hint to others that he knew much more.

It seemed he relished his own place in the mystery.

Deep, deep down, Anton knows what he did that night. Eventually the truth will come out, he would say.

And, of course, there was the whole business with the carwash – the apparent murder confession that had given Captain Laux the leverage to make Van Zyl talk in the first place.

Van Zyl had been quick to play that down as a boast, an ignorant, foolish boast. Bravado. Something to impress a stranger.

"It's like saying 'we went dancing last night'," was how he tried to explain it. "That doesn't mean I danced."

14

LAMBS TO THE SLAUGHTER

B Y LATE APRIL the rains had moved on. The sky would be a flawless blue dome for months now. In the Vaal River, the rapids had shrivelled, exposing pink-grey granite islands that were quickly carpeted with crisp leaves shaken from the woods by a fresh wind and by clambering teams of vervet monkeys. High on the river banks, fish eagles cried to one another and kept watch from bare branches. Soon the temperature would drop below freezing at night. The cold and the contrast with the bright warm days were strong enough to crack the granite boulders that filled Parys' ancient crater.

Marie van der Westhuizen was recovering. Her mother had done as she'd asked that Sunday, and left her in peace in her bedroom for a couple of hours, but her sister's fiancé, Miela, had popped over and had put his head round the door to check on her. Later, she seemed to remember that he'd given her a glass of milk, and that she'd thrown it up on the way in to hospital. It took her two weeks to get the drugs out of her system. But the pain in her heart would not leave. She dreaded the thought of going back to school. Telling her father what had happened seemed impossible.

Samuel's girlfriend, Naledi, was also trying to put her life together, still working on the rubbish dump, dressed these days in a grey tracksuit with a thick woollen hat. One evening she'd come home late to find her shack was on fire. It was too late to save anything inside. She'd waited until the flames had finished, and the corrugated-iron had cooled down, and then she'd salvaged the blackened sheets, before they could be stolen, hurriedly dragging them over to her mother's shack and stacking them there against the wall. Within days the ash black square that marked her old home had been taken over by someone else – a line of wire marking a new boundary. That was the way it worked. At first she'd thought perhaps it was her stove that had caught fire, but some people muttered that maybe it had something to do with Samuel, with the case. She hadn't been following it. Wouldn't have known where to start.

*

Late one afternoon, out at the Weiveld crossroads, standing outside Vicky van der Westhuizen's farm workshop in the shadow of the giant grain silos, Fanie Oosthuizen was the first to spot the approaching convoy and its tail of dust. One or two cars usually meant the Hawks were coming to talk, but four meant trouble, for sure. Maybe they had come for his son, Daniel. Or his brother Johann. Fanie knew he had infuriated the Hawks during the bail hearing with all that stuff about how Laux and Topkin had intimidated and threatened him and his family. Maybe it was time for revenge.

The Hawks knew the short-cuts by now but they still kept a stately, implacable pace, just under the speed limit, as if rebuking the farmers, who all drove like the devil was after them. First they approached the long bridge across the river from the north. On the far side, they turned left along Bree Street and made their way around Parys, past the library, past the farmers' co-operative, and then out towards the dirt road that led to the farms. On their left a cluster of makeshift enclosures where a handful of black farmers from Tumahole kept their sheep and cattle. And soon, on the right, the shacks of the informal settlements.

The convoy drove through the farm gates and came to a halt. Colonel Topkin got out and asked, politely, if Muller van der Westhuizen would step this way for a moment.

Thank God, thought Fanie, as he watched them push Muller into the car. Thank God.

*

On the drive back into Parys, Laux allowed himself to think about the weekend. It was already Thursday. He'd head back to Bloemfontein tomorrow afternoon and lie low. Although, even at home this case seemed to follow him. Strangers, whites, would stop him in the supermarket and ask why he was involved – why don't you forget about two kaffirs being killed? Those guys kill the farmers.

But things were about to change. The fresh-faced youngster sitting in the back seat, son of the richest farmer in the district, looked nothing like the confident son and heir today. He looked more like a scared little boy, a lamb heading to the slaughter.

Early on in their investigation, the Hawks had confiscated the guns of a number of farmers linked to the case. Men like Boeta and Anton protested bitterly – it was another sign that the police were ganging up on them, leaving them unprotected at a time when there was talk in the township of revenge. The Hawks had also confiscated about fifty mobile phones and sent them to the cyber-crime unit at the national police head-quarters in Pretoria for analysis.

Some of the phones had been smashed and many of them had been wiped clean – photos deleted, text messages erased. No sign of any videos. But the experts in Pretoria had dug deep into the phones' memories and had managed to excavate a significant amount of material. The most valuable of which proved to be a trove of WhatsApp voice messages.

Forget Ockert van Zyl, Laux thought, as he listened to the recordings. This was the breakthrough.

"I fucked him up."

The young voice belonged to Muller van der Westhuizen. He sounded flat, matter-of-fact, as he told a friend what he'd just done. From the background rumble, he was presumably in a car. The time and date were the evening of Wednesday, January 6, 2016.

"I punched him in his stomach and in his ribs and kicked and damaged him. I threw him down on an anthill and shit like that. The police are here now and we told them the dogs fucked them up."

And then later:

"I just back home now and I need to put on another shirt because if they catch me fucking covered in blood then I'll probably sleep in jail tonight."

*

A few years earlier, Laux had been chasing a killer in Bloemfontein. Some guy who'd been murdering prostitutes – three or four girls already, Laux recalled. There was evidence to suggest the man was using a car's wheel spanner to beat them to death. When the police finally arrested a possible suspect, Laux played out a hunch. He was interviewing the man in his office, late in the evening. Without warning he pulled out a wheel spanner and placed it on the table between them.

Tell me about this then, Laux said.

The man had confessed on the spot. He was given two life sentences. The spanner was from Laux's own car.

"You've got to bullshit them now and then, tell them you've got a full deck of cards when you've got nothing." That was Laux's view – the bluff, the games were part of what had made him stick to the job all these years, right up to the edge of retirement.

Except this time the Hawks were not bluffing. Muller's texts, and similar messages that were now trickling out of the cyber unit in Pretoria, transformed the investigation. This was no longer about second-hand boasts reported by harassed black farmworkers, or the testimony of a braggart like Ockert van Zyl describing Boeta with his fan-belt whip and Captain Prinsloo with his cattle-prod.

Vows of silence meant nothing now. The Hawks had found a door that appeared to open onto a very different crime scene; one where teenage boys – the privileged sons of the local farming aristocracy – were on a shameless, frenzied rampage.

The Hawks had already charged Wian van der Westhuizen back in February, based on his boasts to several farmworkers.

You've got fuck-all against me, Laux remembered him saying. The arrogant little prick. He'd sworn he hadn't been anywhere near the scene that night.

My father will get me out of this.

Things had changed since then.

Laux had also found out about Wicus' car – the suspension broken, racing across the field that night. One morning at court, he'd asked Wicus to confirm which out of four parked bakkies owned by him and his friends was his.

Which one do you want it to be? Wicus had shot back.

Laux had impounded all four vehicles on the spot. That had made the youngsters sit up.

And now they had the mobile phone records putting Wian in the right location on January 6.

I don't care, Laux had told him. You can go to jail – for someone else's deeds. It's not my life. I'm not the one who is going to do two life sentences for killing two unknown blacks.

Then they picked up Wicus, who'd been lying low in Mozambique but had recently returned home. The cyber-crime unit had unearthed one of his WhatsApp messages from the day of the attack.

"We found the people! Two kaffirs! Don't you worry, we spoke very, very nicely to them," he says to a friend, his voice sly with sarcasm. "They were badly fucked up, hey ... More than just a little bleeding. If a punch is going to kill you then you know you must have been punched fucking hard!"

*

Next the Hawks went north, over the crater and down its long, smooth outside slope to the university town of Potchefstroom, where Anton Loggenberg's son, Cor, was now deputy head boy at the local boarding school, preparing for his final exams. Laux had called to alert the headmaster, who arranged for Cor to be brought to his office after school and taken away in an unmarked car. But Cor's mother, Gusta, was furious – they were treating him like a thief, like a criminal, she complained. Why couldn't the Hawks have just called the parents? No respect. She and Anton would have brought him to the station themselves.

Cor was Gusta's middle child. Strong, devout, polite, not like the other boys, not one to smoke and drink, she always told people. He'd struggled with reading when he was younger. He still had the occasional nightmare, which Gusta thought was connected to a farm attack they'd experienced when he was little. Four black guys at night. She and Anton had gone outside and had left Cor with a shotgun. He was only nine years old. He'd seen one of the men hiding behind a tree. Then there had been the Van Rooyen murder. Cor had been close to the old woman who ended up in the freezer. He still woke up screaming in the night sometimes.

None of that impressed Laux. Another arrogant kid, right from the start. Behaved like his family had all the money in the world. Which wasn't, in fact, the case.

The evening Cor was taken into custody Gusta took a Bible to her son in the cells in Parys. He could hardly stop crying. She said Laux had told him his life was over, that he'd spend the next twenty-five years in jail.

They came for Loedie and Miela that same day. Boeta and Rikki van der Westhuizen's son and their daughter's fiancé were both at Cook's Rest. Laux had been on Loedie's case for a while now – he was the worst of the lot, an arrogant little arsehole, a fighter, just like his dad. They'd even fined him one thousand rand for driving without a licence. This time it was just like the day they'd come for Boeta, after he'd threatened Laux over the phone. A S.W.A.T. team. A big police convoy. The works.

A whole army, Rikki called it. Terrible.

15

MONEY TALKS

THE DOGS WERE out first – two young fox terriers spill-ing from the seat of Anton Loggenberg's white pickup and rushing towards the two men standing in the sunshine at Weiveld farm.

Bloody hell, they're strong!

They're still young. This one is half-calm. It looks like one of Boeta's.

I got them at auction, Anton said, catching up with the dogs and already breathing hard from the exertion.

It was eight in the morning on a fine winter's day, and Anton was on the warpath. He'd heard rumours. Maybe more than rumours. The word on the farms was that someone – perhaps several people – had broken the farmers' vow of silence.

Anton had been trying to get hold of Vicky van der Westhuizen all yesterday, calling his neighbour until late at night, and calling Vicky's brother Neils and their father too. No reply. Typical. He knew they looked down on him, with his small farm, his bankruptcy, and all of the rest of it.

Vicky didn't much like big Anton either. Didn't want to speak to him, and certainly didn't want to be summoned to his house for whatever it was that was so important he had to wake people up at ten at night. Finally, this morning, Vicky had returned Anton's call. He told Anton he'd been at his home on the Parys golf estate, but that he was now at Weiveld farm. If Anton really wanted to speak to him, and to his brother Neils, then now would be a convenient time to come over.

I'm on my way, Anton said.

Vicky knew, or could guess, exactly what was bothering Anton. He knew the fresh rumours that were flitting around the farms. He knew trouble was coming. It couldn't be postponed for much longer.

Ag, you know these fucking stories, Anton, Vicky said when Anton arrived at the farm. A little fucking story here and another one there.

But Anton had had enough of the pleasantries and the beating around the bush.

People are saying that some of the accused have turned state witness, he said. When I heard that I just thought that ... if those stories are going around, then you must know what's going on.

There it was. Almost immediately. A barely disguised accusation from Anton. He was asking Vicky and Neils if their kids had turned into snitches.

Because this thing is going to ... this thing may get ugly, Anton added. It sounded like a threat.

Yes. No. For sure. I mean, uh, look ...

*

The short answer to Anton's question, to his accusation, was – yes.

Almost from the beginning, from that meeting with Kobus

Burger when the lawyer had told the Van der Westhuizen clan that unity and silence were the farmers' best defence, Vicky had been having doubts. Yes, they'd deleted all the photos on their phones, and burned the shoes, the fan-belt and more, and Muller had burned his shirt, and there had been other meetings since. In all of the meetings Anton and Boeta had continued to express their opinion, vehemently, that solidarity was their only option.

But just to be on the safe side, to explore other options, Vicky had hired a different, more cautious lawyer, Jan Ellis, to represent his son Muller, his two brothers' boys, Wicus and Wian, and Vicky's farm staff – brothers Fanie and Johann Oosthuizen and Fanie's son Daniel.

Just to be safe.

And then had come the bombshell of Muller's WhatsApp recordings and his arrest.

At first Vicky had assumed Captain Laux was bluffing him when he called to outline their contents. He knew his son. He hadn't raised Muller like that. He would never say such things. But Laux was emphatic – the voice messages alone were enough for them to hang this whole case around Muller's neck. He would go down for double murder. An eighteen-year-old, carrying the can for everyone.

Or maybe it was time to talk.

Jan Ellis had always been contemptuous of Kobus Burger's strategy of saying nothing, and staying united. People died, he told his new Van der Westhuizen clients. Silence is not an option. The Hawks could charge them with "common purpose" – meaning they could potentially be found guilty of murder just for being at the scene. Now that the WhatsApp messages had been uncovered, any lingering possibility of keeping quiet had been removed.

Ellis came recommended by Kobus Dannhauser, the head of their farmers' union. Ellis was an older man. Solicitous. A far cry from Burger, who was always swearing, always smelling a conspiracy and screaming "Bullshit!"

Of course, Boeta and his boy Loedie were relatives too, but they were one step removed from Vicky's immediate family. Anton's mother had been a Van der Westhuizen – a further step removed. Scratch the surface around here and almost everyone was related. But you had to draw the line some-where – however much trouble it might cause.

*

To tell you the honest truth, Anton—

At Weiveld farm Vicky was still trying to find a way to avoid lying to Loggenberg directly, but it was getting steadily harder.

We weren't even there when it happened, Vicky said.

The less I know, the better, Neils added.

Same for me, Vicky said. I want fuck-all to do with it. Neils was in New Zealand and I was in the Cape. To tell you the honest truth, Anton, Vicky said again, I am shit scared. If I say something wrong, they'll fucking lock me up.

They made me almost shit myself too, Neils said.

We have to be careful, Anton conceded gruffly. These fucking Hawks are trying to cause friction. They want to get someone to start talking. They're trying to make us panic. It's their way, to split us into two camps. We must just fucking stand together. I swear before God that I won't talk. I promise you, when we were in jail we didn't say a fucking word – nothing. The Hawks were getting fuck-all out of anyone until the other day when they arrested Cor and the others.

Vicky said, again, that he was on the side-lines of the whole affair. He had no control over his foreman, Fanie, he admitted – how could he tell a grown man what to say or do? – but he couldn't throw his people to the wolves, could he? Let's just say that Fanie has now turned state witness. I don't *know* if he has, but let's just say he did, then am I going to tell him Listen, you fuck, you can't do this or that?

It was as close to an admission as Vicky felt able to go. The Hawks had told him not to disclose their meetings.

But Anton understood it well enough. He felt emboldened, ready to start getting specific, to talk about who really knew what about the events of that night, and who was lying.

Boeta and I ... we arrived there late. We don't know who beat those boys, and bashed them with spanners and stuff, said Anton. Then he addressed a rumour that had been circulating on the farms. They're saying I jumped on their heads.

Which was nonsense, of course.

With my body, I can't even climb two stairs. How can I fucking jump? And I mean, if *had* jumped on their heads, then it wouldn't have just cracked their fucking skulls. Their eyes would have popped out.

Then he came to the nub of it, to the whole reason he had driven over to Weiveld farm this morning. He wanted to make it clear that if Vicky and Neils' kids and workers started telling their version of events to the Hawks, then that was it. No more Van der Westhuizen solidarity. No more protecting each other.

Or each other's kids, for that matter.

Ask your children if they told you the honest truth about what happened there, Anton said. Because I know the truth about what Boeta did, and what I did, and what Cor did. And there's no fucking way anything we did could have killed those blacks. If it comes to the point where they're putting people in jail, then I'll have no choice but to speak. I won't let my child go away for life.

And if that wasn't clear enough for Vicky and Neils, Anton spelled it out – spelled out what he knew must have happened to the two dead men, what the youngsters – Muller, Wicus and Wian – must have done to them, and where all this was now heading.

I didn't see it with my own eyes, but I heard those blacks were picked up in the air and smashed to buggery on the rocks. I'm saying now that if ribs were broken, and skulls were broken, it was then. And if this thing is going to end in the High Court, then our lawyers will tear the kids apart. I wouldn't want any child to end up in that witness box because it's a fuck-up. Do you hear me?

After delivering the threat, Anton made a final plea for unity.

Vicky, we have to help the children. I will sit in jail if it helps my children. We can't throw those kids away. Their lives will be fucked up for good.

Somehow, that last thought seemed to calm things.

Anton turned to leave.

O.K., Anton. Cheers. Good luck, Vicky said.

That maize is starting to dry.

I've got six hundred and fifty hectares left to harvest.

Anton and his fox terriers got back in the pickup and drove off.

Neils turned to his brother. Did you manage to record it all?

Yes.

Anton might have still been hoping there was a chance to keep the farmers together, but in fact Vicky and his people had already made their move. They had their own lawyer, their own version of events, and before Anton had arrived at the farm that morning, Vicky had taken the precaution of clicking an app on his phone and switching on a voice-recorder.

Just to be on the safe side.

16

THE DEVIL GOT INSIDE ME

BARRY ROUX STROLLED out to the reception area, as he always did, to meet his new clients. He was sixty-one now and eager to put the Oscar Pistorius case – the drawn-out trial, the subsequent appeal, the athlete's murder conviction, the whole mad circus of it all – behind him. Easier said than done. He was a household name now, for better and for worse, and not only in South Africa.

A few days earlier, he'd received a call from an old friend in Potchefstroom. Roux had known Jan Ellis since the late '70s when they'd studied law together. Ellis was three years older and, not for the first time, was looking to his friend for some advice about a difficult case. Roux had heard about the Parys killings on the radio, but not the latest twist. The WhatsApp revelations had not been made public yet. He listened to Ellis sketch out the situation.

For the first consultation in Johannesburg, Vicky van der Westhuizen and his lawyer drove up on their own. Roux ushered them into his second-floor office overlooking the Johannesburg Stock Exchange in Sandton, and they sat down at one end of a long, polished table. A collection of model cars – chubby, painted clay sculptures of taxis, ambulances, buses and their drivers and passengers – competed with law books for space on the shelves.

Roux's advice was neither cheap nor comforting. There was a window of opportunity for Vicky's son and the rest of their group, he said, but it was already closing. Their evidence was only valuable while the Hawks didn't have all the facts. They needed to move fast. Now. If they didn't, then someone else would. In cases like this, eventually someone always talked.

Vicky drove home to Parys, briefed his family and his staff, told them he wasn't going to let his son go to jail, and offered to pay everyone's legal fees. All of them. His foreman, Fanie, leaped at the offer. The way he saw it, this wasn't a bribe for his acquiescence, but a generous gesture from a scrupulously honest employer, someone who'd looked out for him and his family for the past seventeen years.

It was Anton Loggenberg, actually, who had helped him make up his mind. The first time Fanie had seen the big man after the incident was in court, in the dock, at Fanie's bail hearing. Anton had leaned over to him to speak, but not to say hello, not to ask him how he was coping.

Remember when I arrived there, on the scene? Anton said. Remember, everything was already over by then.

Fanie had realised, right there and then, that this talk of solidarity wouldn't last for ever. Maybe Boeta wouldn't break. He'd been straight with everyone so far, just telling them to keep quiet. But Anton …

In the end it would be every man for himself.

Muller, meanwhile, was in tears. It was all his fault. That terrible WhatsApp message – that wasn't the real him. And now they were all breaking ranks, betraying their relatives. What his father was saying to them now meant that he would have to turn against his uncle, Oom Boeta, a man he'd known his entire life.

For their next consultation, a few days later, this time the whole group went to the meeting in Johannesburg with Barry Roux. When they arrived at his Sandton office, Roux put on a bit of a performance. The usual routine – but every word was deliberate. Muller, Wian, Wicus, Fanie and his brother and son, sitting where Oscar Pistorius had once sat, were all a little in awe of this famous lawyer, with his jutting chin, narrowing eyes, and ominous warnings about time lost, about being in a race against other witnesses, about how bloody serious this case was for all of them. They had no idea. They could easily be spending the next fifteen years in prison. It gave them the chills.

Roux explained about being a 204 witness. A state witness. You had to come clean, tell the police everything, because you'd be cross-examined in court, maybe for days, and if, at the end of it, the judge decided that you'd not been entirely honest, then your immunity could be withdrawn and you could be sent to jail.

With that, Roux asked them all to leave the room, and to return, one at a time, to give him their individual version of events. Every detail. The whole truth. Of course there would always be small disparities – human memory worked that way. In fact, too identical a set of statements would attract suspicion, would smack of a conspiracy. And so they began talking.

*

On Weiveld farm on January 6, 2016, Fanie had been out planting mealies, and had popped back to his cottage to get a drink when a call came through on his mobile. Oom Loedie has been attacked.

Jesus!

He went to grab his shotgun, then radioed his brother Johann, who was still out in the fields with Wian, Daniel and Muller. They set off in two cars. On the way, Muller phoned Wicus, who was heading towards Sasolburg to finish spraying some fields on that side. They all agreed to gather, as soon as possible, at Bulrush farm – Oom Loedie's place.

Fanie was thinking about the Van Rooyens. About that freezer. How could he not – he'd been hearing the story for years. You can't take it out of your head. Still, he wasn't setting out to look for revenge – chasing thieves was just one of those things you were expected to do as a foreman. He and his brother could hardly say no to their boss.

Oom Loedie was outside his house, talking to Boeta. You could see the blood shining on his head and chest. Fanie and his brother drove through the yard and on towards the long line of trees at the edge of the farm, to search for the attackers. They'd already heard that there were two of them, or maybe three, and that they had a gun. Wian and Muller searched the mealie fields – standing on top of the car to get a better view. Nothing. The same in the trees. Fanie and Johann turned and drove back towards the barns – big dark wood buildings, full of crates and machinery. They went inside, slowly, someone pointing a torch into the corners. It was unnerving. But again, nothing.

Suddenly, Fanie heard a car revving hard. He went outside just in time to see Wicus shooting off down Oom Loedie's driveway. Fanie and Johann ran to their vehicle and followed. A minute later, Fanie's son, Daniel, called. He said he was with Wicus in his car. The Cilliers had just spotted two blacks running across their farm, Blackstone. And now everyone was racing towards the same spot, texting each other as they converged.

"We found the people. Two kaffirs. We found them!"

Up ahead, Wicus could see the Cilliers' car had already stopped. A second later, he spotted the two black men – one still running, the other being abruptly tackled to the ground. Wicus gunned his car across the field, too fast, a shock absorber shearing off as his front wheel slammed into a hole. He and Daniel jumped out and ran towards a barbed-wire fence, ducking under it, and coming to a breathless stop beside the smaller of the two men.

Wicus recognised the man. He'd done a few weeks work on the farm recently. Was he Samuel? It was hard to remember.

The two young white men charged up to him and kicked him hard, in his ribs. Samuel would have known both of their names. The workers knew all the white farmers' names.

A car door slammed shut. It was Klein Loedie, Boeta's scrappy son, now rushing over and punching Samuel hard in the face.

As Loedie shouted, he crouched down and smashed the wrench into the ground beside Samuel's head, trying to scare him.

"Where's the fucking gun?" Loedie was screaming, running between Simon and Samuel, slapping, kicking and punching them. "What are you doing with my grandfather's dogs?"

They gave no answer. Samuel tried to block the blows.

Then Muller and Wian arrived. All within seconds. It was as if they were trying to outdo each other. Wian – small, wispy bearded Wian – had a knife on his belt, a Leatherman, and he started throwing it hard at Simon's face. Then Loedie rushed back to his car and returned with a long monkey-wrench.

What were you doing at the old man's house?

Muller would recall that he told Loedie to be careful – that he could kill him with a wrench that big. Then Loedie stood up and swung the wrench straight into the side of Simon's head. Wicus saw him do it several times. Almost like a golf swing.

Then, as Simon wriggled and cowered on the ground, Muller and Wian began kicking him. They were aiming for his head but it was hard to catch him properly. Muller went back over to Samuel and picked him up by his belt and shirt collar. This was the moment he'd boast about later – about throwing him "down on an anthill and shit like that". In the version he gave to the police, Muller pulled Samuel up to his own waist height, then half dropped him, half pushed him back down, leaning over and pinning him to the ground with his weight. His cousins described it in exactly the same way.

Johan Cilliers, the farmer's son who'd been first on the scene, remembered it a little differently. He said Muller had picked up one of the suspects, more than once, and thrown him to the ground, and then Wian had put his foot on the man's face. Johan had called him over and told him to stop, and to tell the others to stop too.

Fanie Oosthuizen had no problem with a little violence. A

slap or a kick. It's not like you don't like the blacks but ...
Jesus! Sometimes it's difficult with them. When Fanie and his
younger brother Johann arrived by the trees a few minutes
later, Klein Loedie was still kicking one of them.

Then Muller's mobile rang. It was his father, in Cape Town,
wanting to know what had happened, and telling his boy
he didn't want any shit. No more violence, Vicky van der
Westhuizen said.

Fanie asked his brother to tell Loedie and the others to
calm down. They'd made their point. Not that the youngsters
would do what he or Johann asked. No way. The two blacks
were still conscious, still talking, no sign of blood on them.

Fanie went over to the taller suspect, the one in the T-shirt,
and asked him where the gun was. No answer. So Fanie
grabbed him by the arm, wrapping his own arm under it and
using his other arm to bend it down, from the elbow, the
wrist, even from the finger, towards the ground. It was an old
policeman's trick.

Where's the gun?

We threw it away.

Where did you throw it?

No answer. Fanie bent his elbow back harder.

No, Fanie, you're hurting me! Please, baas Fanie.

Fanie stopped and looked at Simon. So this one knew his
name. He supposed he must have come across him somewhere
over the years but he wasn't good with the names or even with
their faces. It was enough that they all knew him – Vicky van
der Westhuizen's foreman. Still, now he'd have to be careful.
The blacks would steal the diesel, steal a sheep, steal ten sheep,

steal tools at work, and nothing would happen. You could call the police. Still nothing would happen. But if you gave someone a slap, then thirty minutes later there would be two police vans at your door. It was maddening.

A month earlier, there had been warnings about a possible farm attack in the area – a group of blacks from Sasolburg. Maybe some sort of crime syndicate. A couple of days later, Fanie had spotted a small car parked on the road near the grain silos and when he'd gone over to investigate, he'd found a man hiding in the foot-well on the passenger side. He'd dragged him out and called the police. This time they'd actually arrived quickly and found credit cards and cash and phones in the car – maybe sometimes they did do their jobs.

Leave them alone. The police are coming, Fanie now said to the others in the field. It wasn't worth the risk. It was enough that they'd caught them. He went over to the shorter man, who was sitting on the ground, watching him. Fanie's son, Daniel, had been swearing at Samuel – said he'd got his shoes on, that he must have stolen them from work. He'd kicked him in the groin and on the legs. Now Fanie crouched down beside Samuel and asked him about the gun. No reply. Fanie grabbed his hand and bent his finger back sharply.

Why did you hit Oom Loedie?

No, we went looking for work. The old man told us to leave. He chased us away.

That's what Fanie recalled Samuel answering.

Did you have a gun?

No reply. Then Fanie's brother came over. He grabbed

Samuel's arm, pulled him up, and punched him in the stomach. Samuel doubled over and crumpled back to the ground.

I'm sorry, Samuel said.

Why did you attack the old man?

We didn't. He was the one who hit us, with a broomstick. It snapped and hit him on his head.

That was where all the blood had come from.

When Fanie had finished, Wicus tried talking to Samuel in Sesotho, asking him why he'd done it, why he'd attacked the old man.

I don't know. The devil got inside me. I don't know why. I'm sorry.

That was how Wicus recalled Samuel's answer.

Fanie had seen that devil plenty of times. The anger, the hostility that could flare up without warning, especially in the township. Even from kids – tiny kids – who would throw stones at the pickup, trying to puncture the tyres, when he went to pick up the workers. You could feel the hatred coming off them like a flame.

But this business with Oom Loedie was complicated. In the months to follow, and as the farmers' unity began to splinter, Fanie would find himself siding with Captain Laux's theory about the attack – that maybe there hadn't been a gun after all, that two young, strong guys like Simon and Samuel would surely have overpowered an old man, would have killed him if they'd wanted to, rather than running away with the dogs as they'd done. And what the suspect had said, about Oom Loedie fighting back with the broom – there was a logic lurking there.

All this time, more cars were arriving in the corner of the rutted field. Boeta van der Westhuizen's daughter, Crista, turned up with Miela, her fiancé.

Today we're going to do some shooting, Miela said, quickly catching the mood and striding over to kick Samuel in the stomach, while Loedie trampled on his head. Still, Fanie would later insist, at this stage neither of the blacks was looking too bad. They could still talk, still sit up, still breathe just fine.

And then another pickup drove in, fast, not stopping like the others but driving straight towards one of the suspects. Loedie and Miela had to grab him and pull him out of the way. Just in time. It was Boeta. In a fury.

Now the trouble is really going to start, Fanie heard someone say.

*

And that was, more or less, how Vicky van der Westhuizen's group chose to remember their part in the drama.

They'd all done wrong. They were all were guilty of assault. No question about it.

Samuel and Simon had been roughed up – you could understand the youngsters were angry, had every reason to be angry – but that was all.

There were a few discrepancies in their versions, but nothing substantial, they'd made sure of that.

17

TRAITORS

WHERE'S MY TOOTHBRUSH? Elias asked in the dark of the shack. Lawrence slid off their double bed, walked groggily past his brother towards the door, and lifted the puppy, Romeo, out of his basket. Ruth was already dressed, had cleared her sleeping things off the floor, and was standing outside in the cold, hungrily smoking a cigarette and waiting for the sun to come up over the bristled mealie field behind.

For months she'd felt cursed. It wasn't just Samuel's death. It was what she'd said to the journalists after that first day in court – about not working for her enemy and other angry things. Ruth thought that was why she hadn't been able to find a new job, that all the white people in the region had seen her on television and wouldn't hire her. She thought about the biscuits she used to bake at this time of year on La Rochelle farm, for Mercia and Hector to take to the church bazaar. It hadn't been such a bad life.

Recently, a relative up the road in Vanderbijlpark had hired Ruth to look after his grandmother and a two-year-old boy. The child's mother was working nights, and the father had a job down in Durban. The pay was one thousand rand a month, and nothing extra for transport. Ruth enjoyed cleaning. In my heart, she'd say, I'm a woman who can't live in a dirty house.

It wasn't quite an obsession, but cleaning had been such a big part of her life for so long that she would scan an appraising eye over any room she entered.

But this job was too much. The old woman was blind and couldn't look after herself. Ruth had to clean up the excrement. Eish. I know I'm poor, she told a visitor, but I'm not a dog. She added her usual chuckle. At home the electricity was still off, and at the place she worked the power would cut off unexpectedly in the winter and she'd get trapped behind the electric gate and have to stretch out an arm and ask passers-by to fetch her a cigarette from the kiosk at the end of the road.

At least Elias was finding work now. He'd had a couple of months packing mushrooms for some Chinese businessmen, then a gardening job for a white man, and now he had a regular income at an abattoir in Sasolburg, six days a week. He seemed to have changed his ways. Ruth had given him a big lecture a while back – Open your eyes! she'd shouted at him. If you do bad things they'll come around again, you'll end up behind bars. Elias had two young sons, her grandsons, with different women, one in Parys, the other down the road in a place called Koppies. Lawrence, meanwhile, was treading water. He talked about getting a C.V. printed in town, but he'd been planning that for months and nothing had come of it yet.

Ruth had kept a handful of photographs of Samuel, but in April the rain had leaked through the shack and now the pictures were cracked and peeling. You could still see him clearly, that wide grin, lounging with friends on a couch, or in the shade after one of the weekend football matches they sometimes played on the farms, or hunched over a kerosene stove down in Cape Town when he'd gone off to work on the railways. That was long after he'd quit school to get a job at La Rochelle to help the family out. After that, he and Lawrence had gone to work at a coal mine near Koppies, then another job somewhere near Pretoria. Samuel had finally come home, sick, after going to hospital for an appendix operation.

One day he told his mother he'd had enough, that he couldn't live like this, shuffling from one job to the next, never getting anywhere.

*

The trees in the neat little courtyard outside the magistrate's court in Parys were bare and the dry grass so pale it looked almost like snow. For months, the farmers had gathered here ahead of each bail appearance, sitting in the shade on a low brick wall, sharing sandwiches or biltong. But now they were divided in two distinct groups. It had happened without a word being said.

Rikki van der Westhuizen stood beside her husband Boeta, feeling like the world had just turned upside down again. They'd all heard the rumours about Muller and the others becoming 204s – state witnesses. Vicky had as much as admitted it to Anton. But until this morning, Rikki had hoped it might all be a mistake. Then she'd seen them standing to one side, in a little circle, over towards the police station, and there could be no doubt left. Then Muller, Wian, Fanie and the rest of them were joined by Captain Laux and Colonel Topkins. They weren't even pretending to keep it a secret.

Boeta sat down on the wall. The little hair he'd once had

was just about gone, just a few grey strands left. His face sagged into his neck. Jesus, he'd been fit once – inside centre on the rugby field and fast! Now he seemed trapped in concrete, his speech as slow as his movements.

Nothing was official yet but it didn't need to be.

Just look at them. Traitors.

I don't know why. I don't know why, Boeta said flatly, glancing over at the other group. They're my nephews.

Boeta had spent a month in jail for making that threatening call to Captain Laux before the Appeal Court in Bloemfontein had overturned the decision to revoke his bail and he'd been released. The judge had been contemptuous of the Hawks' behaviour and today the prosecution was officially withdrawing the intimidation charges against him.

Rikki had brought snacks. She began handing them out – to her boy, Loedie, and to Miela, Crista's fiancé, who already seemed like a second son. She thought about the future. What if she met the 204s, or their families, on the street, or in church? Could she look them in the eye? And what about the holiday weekend she had been planning with Wicus' parents, Neils and Rose. They were – they'd been – such close friends. Now they'd have to cancel the trip to Sun City. They'd made their choice.

Maybe it was the shock of it, but Rikki felt like the repercussions of this day would last for decades, or longer, the bitterness passed on from one generation to the next like some feud from the Boer War. Perhaps the Van der Westhuizens would never recover.

At least Marie seemed to be doing better. After she had been discharged from hospital she had gone to stay with the neighbours, with Tannie Gusta – Anton Loggenberg's wife – for a few weeks. Marie didn't want to go back home just yet, but she had eventually plucked up the courage to tell her father what had happened, before he heard it on the grapevine. Boeta had broken down and sobbed.

I'm so sorry I ruined your life, he'd said to his daughter.

It wasn't you. It wasn't your fault, Marie told him.

Anton Loggenberg was also sitting on the wall outside the court. The friendship he and Boeta had shared since school had never extended to their wives. They didn't really visit each other as families. Gusta told people that Rikki was her neighbour, not her friend, and when she was feeling particularly frank, she'd go as far as saying that Rikki and Boeta were racists – that her own workers had confided in her about the way Boeta hit them, the way he spoke to them, and underpaid them. And that whole business with the sausages, yes, she'd heard about that and thought maybe that really was the trigger for all this. By contrast, Gusta said, their workers loved her – all the black people loved her. She understood the way they thought. It helped that she spoke good isiXhosa; and Anton spoke Sesotho as well as anyone.

For her part, Rikki preferred not to talk about the Loggenbergs. That was how she usually handled confrontation – quietly. We ... we get along, she would say, with a small smile. But no, I don't like Gusta's sharp tongue. Let's leave it at that.

There was something else that bound the neighbours together – a shared experience of financial stress. Two bad harvests in a row. Then the last drought. They had been in serious trouble. And now this case. The financial cost of it was one thing, but the dawning realisation of what was happening to their precious sons – Klein Loedie and Cor Loggenberg – was something else altogether. The boys had been arrested solely because their friends, their cousins, had broken ranks, betrayed the collective and pinned the killings on them. And wasn't it a convenient coincidence that the evidence had split so neatly – that Boeta and his son and their neighbours were the ones who'd killed those two men; that all the kicks and punches delivered by those on Vicky's side of the Van der Westhuizen family, and his workers, had barely left a mark?

The new magistrate was late arriving. It was almost noon before the families headed inside to the courtroom. So many delays. So many of these brief, pointless hearings. Whatever this was, it didn't feel like justice.

*

Magistrate Pillay was still at work. She had spent the morning rattling through a dozen minor cases, including one involving the E.F.F. who'd tried to occupy some land not far from the graveyard in Tumahole. It had ended up in a scrap with the police. Now the E.F.F. were challenging a separate court order against some of their members, one of whom was the indomitable Paul, which barred them from going anywhere near the town hall, which meant they couldn't go to collect their social grants. Pillay smiled, shook her head, and suggested to Paul that he try going into the town hall on his own, and quietly.

The last case in front of Pillay that morning – before she made way for her replacement in the farm murder case – involved a young white man called Eric, who'd been standing outside chatting with the 204s. A court orderly came out onto the steps and shouted his name.

"Drunk driving," Muller said with a grin.

18

DIE, DOG, DIE

THE TRAFFIC-CLOGGED motorway that snakes south from Sandton cuts into the heart of Johannesburg, carving and surfing its way through and over a series of steep ridges before settling down and emptying out for the long, lonely drive to the Free State, with its ponderous hills and vast horizons.

It is a curious fact that the biggest of those urban ridges – the one that ruffles the northern edge of Johannesburg like a buckled carpet – is another product of Parys' ancient meteorite strike. The ridge marks the outer edge of the geological ripples produced by that world-shuddering collision. Perhaps more significantly, that same impact pushed a thin seam of gold deep underground, protecting it from later upheavals that would, ordinarily, have seen it washed into the ocean. Instead, the buried seam crept to the surface near the outer ridge, to be discovered in the nineteenth century, prompting the gold rush that helped to establish Johannesburg and, along with it, a system of racial segregation designed by white businessmen anxious to ensure a steady supply of cheap black labour to chase the gold seam back – nearly four kilometres – underground.

Barry Roux set off early. It was a clear morning as he headed south on the N1 motorway. He noted the Parys turn-off but sped past it, on to Bloemfontein, roughly a four-hour drive from the City of Gold. He had with him a thick folder of documents – the separate statements he'd compiled in his Sandton office from each member of Vicky van der Westhuizen's group: Muller, Wian and Wicus van der Westhuizen, brothers Fanie and Johann Oosthuizen, and Fanie's son Daniel. In Bloemfontein, he had a meeting set up with Vicky and his lawyer, Jan Ellis, at the National Prosecuting Authority's offices, where they would show the compilation to the prosecutor, J.J. Mlotshwa, and play him the WhatsApp voice messages.

Vicky hadn't heard Muller's voice messages yet. He was still unwilling to believe how damning they were.

The men were shown to Mlotshwa's office. Once greetings were over. Mlotshwa invited them to take a seat. Colonel Topkin and Captain Laux were already there.

Then the WhatsApp recordings were played for the visitors.

"I fucked him up … threw him down on an anthill and shit like that …"

It was, indeed, as damning as they'd been told.

O.K., Barry Roux said, how can we sort this issue out?

Laux recalled Roux then putting some documents on the table and saying to the prosecutor: Look, I'll make it simple for you. Here are the statements from my clients. All off the record, for now. Take a look at them. See whether you think there's anything for us to discuss, whether you're interested in taking my clients as 204s.

The prosecutor took the documents into another room and began reading.

*

Now the trouble is really going to start.

Now comes the big trouble.

It was something like that anyway. If not the actual words, they'd all remembered the tone of the voice – half threatening, half joking – announcing the arrival of Anton and Boeta, the two men's pickups roaring towards the corner of the field, one behind the other.

And it was true, what they all said in their statements. That really was when everything had turned properly ugly.

Boeta had charged straight over to Simon – his former worker, the fucker who'd stolen meat from him, the one he'd beaten more than once at his farm before sacking him. Simon was slouched on his left side. Boeta began punching him, kicking, shouting, demanding to know where the gun was. His son, Loedie, out of breath from all the exertion he'd already put in, joined in.

What the fuck were you doing with the old man?

No answer.

Where's the fucking gun?

Simon was trying to block the blows. Sorry, baas, sorry, baas.

Boeta turned away from Simon for a second.

Bring me a gun!

He was shouting at Harvey Coetzee, one of the other farmers' boys, who had brought his father's .38 revolver along without permission. Boeta snatched hold of it, crouched down again over Simon's body, and pushed the barrel into his forehead.

If you don't tell me where the gun is, I'm going to shoot.

No, Boeta! No! Don't!

It was Boeta's daughter, Crista, screaming at her father. The others turned to look.

Don't shoot! shouted Miela.

Think what you're doing! Muller called out. Wian too.

Wicus, Fanie and the rest of them watched Boeta as he swivelled his gun, so that he was then holding it by the barrel. He began swinging it down, smashing the wood and metal butt hard into Simon's face. How many times? No-one seemed sure, but a good few; they could see the blood flowing, and Simon no longer trying to block the blows, slumping back, flat on the ground, maybe unconscious.

The gun had come apart in Boeta's hands. Loedie picked it up and laughed, showing it to his friends. Want to see what a broken revolver looks like? he said. It's fucked up.

Next it was the Loggenbergs' turn. Anton had brought his pickup right up beside the two suspects. That way, with his enormous bulk, he wouldn't have to walk too far. His boy, Cor, had hardly waited for the vehicle to stop moving before he jumped out. He reached back inside the cab and pulled out a walking stick – a thick bamboo kierie.

Samuel had been sitting, his knees tucked up by his chest, watching Boeta interrogate his friend. Now Cor strode towards him, he had a prefect's swagger to him, brandishing the stick. He didn't say a word.

Crack!

They all remembered the sound it made striking Samuel's shins. Fanie thought the bone must have snapped, it was that loud and that hard. He was standing nearby and had to duck to avoid getting hit.

Nice. He wanted that, Anton said approvingly, walking over. He spoke briefly to Samuel in Sesotho.

Cor swung the kierie a few more times, then Anton told him to go and find a rope.

Some of the other farmers exchanged uncomfortable glances. A rope? What next? Was it just to tie them up, or were the Loggenbergs planning to drag the suspects behind their bakkie? This was getting out of hand.

By this time the Cilliers father and son had left, gone to look for Oom Loedie's dogs – there was talk they were bothering the sheep in a nearby field. No-one seemed willing to tell Boeta or Anton to take it easy. Someone shrugged and said it was too late for that. Boeta was in a fury – after all, it was his father who'd just been attacked. Anton was another matter. But look at the way they were both encouraging their sons to join in. That told you all you needed to know about those families. Not like Muller's and Wicus' fathers, Vicky and Neils, who had already been on the phone – angry – ordering their boys not to lay another finger on the two men.

Now came the moment that all the 204s would recall, queasily but almost identically. The moment, the action, that Anton would later insist would have been physically impossible for a man of his size to have done.

As Samuel lay on the ground, his face twisted to one side,

Anton lifted a foot and trampled, again and again, on his head. With his other foot on the ground to steady him, he transferred all his weight, in a grunting, shuffling stamp, onto Samuel's skull. After that, Samuel lay as quiet and still as Simon.

By this time it was deep dusk. A dancing web of departing headlight beams picked out the fence, the trees, a few termite mounds, and a thinning forest of bare legs and khaki shorts. Anton told the youngsters to put the two suspects into the back of his pickup. It was hard work. Muller got blood on his shoulder, and Miela got some on his shoe.

Johann Oosthuizen laughed and still asked them if they were injured and joked that, if so, they needed to take care they didn't catch A.I.D.S.

In the growing darkness, with the motorway falling quiet, and the farmers nodding their goodbyes and heading home in convoy, Anton, Boeta and a few others gathered around the back of Anton's pickup. They could see a police van bumping over the rough ground towards them. Anton looked at Simon, who was lying near the tail gate.

Die, dog, die, he said.

*

Kobus Burger was in his usual seat, out on the Mike's Kitchen veranda in Klerksdorp, smoking more than he knew he should, but to hell with that. One more rum and Coke perhaps, then he'd be off home. Burger had been a prosecutor here; now he was surely the town's most prominent defence lawyer, a bullish man with a penchant for conspiracy theories, large and small, and the genial conviction that South Africa, and the world at large, was going to the dogs.

His wife had gone to school in Parys. She'd been in the same year as Rikki and Gusta, and was even related, in a convoluted way, to the Van der Westhuizens. Burger had grown up on a farm outside Klerksdorp, a town made famous, like Johannesburg, by its gold rush, and by its role in the Boer War and, more recently than the war, as the birthplace of Archbishop Desmond Tutu.

Burger's mobile rang – the sound of Abba's "Dancing Queen" half muffled by his pocket.

If only the farmers had listened to him. From the start he'd told them they should stick together.

You don't turn on each other, he'd insisted. You just don't. If the state can prove its case, let them. But we're not here to help them. We're here to create doubt. If the judge thinks everybody is lying, then everybody goes home. First prize! Don't you think?

The stuff about him telling the youngsters to delete any photos was bullshit. He was a professional, twenty-eight years in the law. That was just the prosecution trying to use their 204s to rattle him, but they'd regret it. As for Barry Roux, Burger knew him well, had come up against him plenty of times as a regional prosecutor and, shall we say, things had seldom gone Roux's way. Maybe he was still smarting from the Pistorius case. Whatever. The bottom line was that the prosecution team were crooks. Remember what the judge in Bloemfontein had said about Boeta's bail appeal, about the way the Hawks had threatened Fanie and assaulted the black farmworkers? Burger was convinced they'd already found the gun too, in the water tank, and had quietly got rid of it because they didn't want it to look like a farm attack. And now, for sure, they'd be trying to cook up the 204 statements to pin everything on his clients – Boeta and Loedie van der Westhuizen, Crista's fiancé Miela, Anton Loggenberg and his son Cor, and Captain Henk Prinsloo – when it was blindingly obvious that the people who'd turned state witness were the ones who'd picked the black men up, thrown them down on stones, broken their bodies. They'd done the bulk of it.

But that was just fine – in fact it would play to their advantage in court.

Do they think we're stupid? Burger wondered out loud. With one brain cell? Imbeciles?

The truth, he knew, was that this case was about politics. Pure and simple. White farmers were under attack in South Africa, and not in some random, criminal way. Not at all. It was an organised campaign to get them off the land, to blame them for the failures of the A.N.C. government. Burger had seen it in court – there would always be a police reservist, or someone like that, involved in the attacks. And there was always torture. Burger himself was no racist – after all, he'd grown up playing with black kids on the farm – but now, as he saw it, their own people were stealing everything. It was getting worse and worse, for everyone. So the politicians were blaming the whites, and a trial like this one in Parys was a useful part of that. It was like that coffin case that had just begun – two white farmers accused of putting a black worker in a coffin to scare him. The media had leaped on that, made a huge deal out of it. But what about the woman – a widow living on her own further north, over the crater's edge towards Johannesburg – who'd been robbed and tortured? The thieves had taken her own electric drill and drilled through her feet, calling her a white bitch. Why would you do that? It's hatred towards the whites, because they once had all these privileges before 1994. In fact, it was only a few who'd really had privileges. Burger had had to pay his own university fees.

Take my word for it, Burger said, as he often did, as if that would prove his point. Take my word for it.

So now the prosecution had its 204 witnesses. They'd all be lying, all of them, to protect Muller van der Westhuizen. After all, it was his father, Vicky, who was paying the lawyers' bills.

This case is war, Burger declared. Straight out war. Nothing more.

19

THEY WERE BLOOD

A S THE VAAL River curves towards Parys from the north east, it splits into two branches. The upper section is broad and rocky; the lower stream is narrower and fast. It gushes through the woods, past the town's sewage treatment plant and the White Giraffe River Cottage, then swings back up to re-join the main branch just beyond a narrow footbridge. The Parys suspension bridge, built in 1919 and recently refurbished by local businesses, once led directly from the town onto a big idyllic island. In a nod towards Paris and a famous pedestrian bridge over the River Seine, its wire sides are covered with thousands of padlocks, some of them rusting, almost all marked with the names of couples – Richard and Aimee, Oscar and Renata – and with hearts.

These days the far end of the footbridge is boarded up, and the island itself has been turned into a private luxury estate, renamed Golf Island. A poster by the concrete steps warns visitors not to feed the monkeys.

Wealthier farmers like Vicky van der Westhuizen, a few local lawyers, and retired businessmen from Johannesburg – lured by the scenery and by Parys' reputation (enhanced by the idea of living within a wind-sheltering crater) for clement weather – own homes in the well-manicured estate. Over the years, several of Simon and Samuel's township friends picked up casual work on the island as gardeners or security guards.

From the bridge it is a fifteen-minute, zig-zagging walk due south across Bree Street and through town to Parys' primary and high schools, each occupying a large suburban block on either side of Schilbach Street. The high school – motto, Each to His Own – is no longer segregated in the old-fashioned sense, but the class photographs in the dark hallways reveal the extent to which language now performs a similar function. Afrikaans for the whites. English for the blacks. Many of Tumahole's new elites – politicians, civil servants, teachers, police – send their children here to be educated by what remains an exclusively white teaching staff, something which the current headmaster suspects may be "part of the appeal".

Magistrate Pillay had put her daughters in the primary school and was astonished to discover it was still named after H.F. Verwoerd, the former South African prime minister and architect of apartheid.

In the winter months of 2016, the head girl at Parys High School was struggling with her health. Alicia Prinsloo, a gentle, forthright, scholarly figure, had been to see doctors and a psychiatrist; she had even been hospitalised before she was diagnosed with stomach ulcers and then with shingles – a nervous disorder brought on, certainly, by the stress of her father's upcoming murder trial.

After Captain Prinsloo's arrest, Alicia and her younger sister, Arne, who was a keen musician and singer, had avoided school for a week. When they returned, the senior boys were still showing each other pictures of the scene on their mobile phones, some of them bragging about what they'd done. The girls could hear the chatter everywhere. It seemed like half the farmers' sons at school had been in the mealie field that night, or at least claimed they'd been there. As head girl, Alicia had felt a duty to control herself, to hide her feelings, but at times she'd just cracked, crying in class, shouting at friends, walking out without permission. It was very unlike her.

One boy had told Arne that his father had been there and knew Captain Prinsloo was innocent.

Yeah, I know he's innocent. Thanks. So why doesn't your father go to the police and tell them?

No, he says he doesn't want trouble.

Alicia stopped talking to any of the boys who'd been involved. The same with their girlfriends. She just wanted the chatter to stop. But some of the teachers would still come over to ask about the trial, about what would happen, as if they wanted to gossip, as if they couldn't just read it in the paper.

In town, people kept stopping their mother, Rona, and telling her, "It's going to be O.K." Rona couldn't bear it. What if it wasn't going to be O.K.? She'd been born in Parys, knew everyone here, was always in and out of the shops because of her job managing supplies at a conference centre nearby. But now she just wanted them all to leave her alone.

She began saying she hated the farmers, hated the white people. Because it was those farmers who had made this happen. Not the black people. We get more support from them, from those who know Henk, she would say. They give us a hug and ask how we're doing.

Rona found comfort in crying. I'm allowed to cry – just

leave me alone. And she'd talk to God in the car, driving around praying, asking Him to keep them safe, to keep them strong, to stop all the stress from just building and building.

The Prinsloos had been a few months away from paying off a twenty-year mortgage on their house. Now they were having to re-mortgage it to pay for Henk's lawyer – and that was before the trial had even started. The money they'd saved for Alicia's university fees was also disappearing. The state had been happy to foot the bill for President Zuma with all his legal problems, but twice now Captain Prinsloo and his lawyer had asked the police to support him financially in his case, and twice they'd refused. Instead they'd transferred him away from Parys to a desk job in Sasolburg, and it hadn't been very long before he was asked to surrender his position on the development committee of the national bowls organisation – Bowls South Africa – because it didn't look good for the sport's image. Her husband's life – his whole family's life – was on hold.

*

Three weeks after Barry Roux had gone to Bloemfontein to hear the WhatsApp messages and to hand over his clients' statements, the prosecution telephoned to announce its decision.

We have a deal, J.J. Mlotshwa said.

No haggling, no complications.

Vicky's son Muller, his two brothers' sons, Wicus and Wian, and his farmworkers Fanie, Daniel and Johann Oosthuizen, would all get 204 status in return for their evidence against the remaining six accused. These were Boeta van der Westhuizen, his son Loedie, and his daughter's fiancé Miela; Anton Loggenberg and his son Cor; and Captain Henk Prinsloo.

It struck some as more than a little odd that the prosecution had agreed to accept all of Vicky's group as 204s. Why not just take Muller? And maybe one extra. Why let the rest of them off the hook so easily? Why not compel them all to plead guilty to aggravated assault – they'd already confessed to that, at the very least – in return for lenient sentences? Then the state would already have a set of convictions in the bank before turning its attention to the other six accused. Come to think of it, why not just put everyone at the scene on trial, and let the judge work out who did what to whom?

Captain Laux acknowledged that the state was taking a big risk. Not that it was his call to make. The 204s could prove to be unreliable, unconvincing witnesses. They might incriminate one another further at trial under cross-examination. But that was the way it worked with 204s: you sacrificed a few suspects to get to the kingpins. And Boeta and Anton were, Laux was adamant, the main guys.

The accused saw things differently. Anton's wife Gusta was sure that money had changed hands, that Vicky had insisted on an all-or-nothing deal for his people. One morning she stopped for a coffee in town at the Spur, the same restaurant her husband had gone to the morning after the incident. She sat alone in a booth, her sharp chin jutting out over the coffee cup, her hair in a neat blonde bob, a pronounced indentation on the bridge of her nose, as if she'd once been punched, hard, in the face. She wore her pearl earrings and a blue nylon shirt with a badge on it saying "Learn, Practise, Play", from the company she worked for that taught sport to the younger kids at some of the local schools. The Loggenbergs were a sporty family – their youngest daughter was on the national squash team.

Gusta had met Anton in 1990 when she went up to Potchefstroom for a sakkie-sakkie dance. He'd been sitting at a table drinking beer, had looked over and seen only the back of her, and had turned to his friends and declared: I am going to marry that girl. Then he'd asked her to dance.

Anton was a year older than Gusta and already a farmer – one of four farming Loggenberg brothers – having dropped out of school after his father died. He was a strong personality, always laughing (but not funny, Gusta would say, in her abrupt manner). Parys was a small town in those days. No Spur, no K.F.C., no pubs to speak of, no retirement homes. Just mealies and cattle. The couple had three children in short order and they still lived in the same farmhouse Anton had grown up in – a brick single-storey home with a lawn adorned with plastic sculptures of Anton's beloved white Brahman cattle. They were just a few kilometres along the road from Boeta and Rikki van der Westhuizen.

Now the family was nearly broke, once again, because of the drought.

Gusta found herself walking through town, pointedly ignoring the nods and hellos of the wives of the 204s. She would catch their eye, for sure, but then she would just stare straight through them. They don't have any heart for us, she thought. But there was more to it than that. This was about money. This was about the wealthy side of the Van der

Westhuizen family ganging up on the poor side. Everyone knew how rich Vicky van der Westhuizen was. The Hawks had been observed, more than once, visiting Vicky at his house on Golf Island.

Lots of farmers had done well from the maize crop and the money was going to their heads. The Van der Westhuizens ran the town – they thought they could do what they wanted – but there were two sides to the family.

Vicky must have paid Captain Laux to get his children out of trouble, Gusta decided; must have paid a lot of money. They didn't feel sorry for others, as long as they were clean. They had paid Laux and everybody to be quiet. Laux was cheeky like that.

It was, as Anton's lawyer, Kobus Burger, had put it, total bullshit. The Hawks were there, on that golf estate, braaiing and partying.

I have suspicions of corruption by police officials, Burger said. They have concocted the 204 statements – that's Mlotshwa's way of doing it. I was quite a prosecutor myself, but I didn't do it this way. You do not bend the facts.

*

It was a while now since the youngsters had gathered at Crista and Miela's place for their Wednesday evening meal. The first time Muller, Wian and Wicus had stayed away, the others had wondered if it meant anything. Then another week came and went, without even a phone call, and the suspicions hardened.

And then suddenly there were those two groups standing apart outside the courthouse, and everyone knew what had happened.

I'm not angry, Crista told Muller when she finally called him. But why aren't you at least talking to us? It felt like a double betrayal. Muller said that the lawyers had told them they couldn't speak to anyone about what they'd done – about giving their statements. And besides, they were simply scared their friends might be – would be – angry with them.

Cor Loggenberg had gone back to school to finish his exams. He'd written an English essay about what it felt like to be in jail. He decided he would contact Muller and tell him he forgave him, but also to let him know he would never be his friend again, would never braai with him again, didn't want anything from any of them now.

Crista tried to forgive Muller. She even began talking to him again, after a while. But not about the case. She didn't need to know what his side was saying, what his version was, and she certainly wasn't going to let him know their own plans.

Klein Loedie, Crista's brother, seemed to be taking it hard. He would hardly speak to his father anymore. Rikki couldn't get through to him either; she felt he'd put up a mask. All those kids who used to come hurtling through her kitchen, so full of life … now her son's closest friends had vanished. It felt like the whole family was grieving. And Marie … It was a lot to process, for all of them. Loedie had already left school early, turning his back on Rikki's hope that he might become an engineer rather than a farmer. Now he was drinking a lot, like his father, and then driving home from town. Rikki was worried about his dark moods, about what he might do.

'Ja, but it's sad,' she said. These kids with their whole lives ahead of them. It was all sad.

One evening Loedie went into Parys for a few beers. He was sitting downstairs at the bar at the Cherry on Top with a couple of friends. Plenty had already turned their backs on him, just to be safe. They were putting it away fast – beers, then Red Heart rum. Upstairs, on the open terrace that looked out over a sharp bend on Bree Street and on towards Golf Island, a party was starting. It was a Van der Westhuizen party, a birthday bash for another of Vicky's boys, Muller's brother Jacob, who'd just turned eighteen. Loedie had been invited. Or maybe he hadn't. Maybe that was the point. It was hard to be sure these days. Anyway, there was no way he was going to mingle with that crowd now.

The Cherry on Top was a casual place. Not like some of those other restaurants on the river bank that had a reputation for using a dress code to keep things smart – and mostly white. Motorbike groups, heading down from Johannesburg and out towards the dirt roads around the crater's edge, would some-times stop there for pizzas and burgers. At weekends the staff would have to watch out for the under-eighteens from the farms, who got angry if they were refused alcohol. The bar-man had been observing Loedie's mood swings for months. Not exactly looking for trouble, but he'd become more thin-skinned, stressed. He hadn't been barred from the place like some other youngsters, but he was someone to keep an eye on.

There must have been about thirty people upstairs – Van

der Westhuizen parents, kids and friends – by the time Loedie changed his mind.

It started with some swearing; Loedie wandering into the crowd, looking for the people who'd betrayed him. He spotted his uncle Vicky and within seconds they were grabbing each other by the shirt, by the throat, shoving each other like two rugby players emerging from a scrum. The other adults quickly clustered round, begging Loedie to calm down, to take this downstairs, to take it outside. But Loedie wanted to make his point – that he knew what Muller and the rest of them had done. They had been there from start to finish and had seen it all, every punch, every kick. Did Vicky know what his boys had really done? Had Muller told his father the truth? Or maybe Vicky didn't want to hear the truth; maybe he just wanted to buy his way – his family's way – out of this mess?

They bundled Loedie back downstairs but the swearing and shouting continued. In the days that followed everyone in town was talking about the big fight at the Cherry on Top, about how open warfare had erupted within the Van der Westhuizen clan. In truth, it wasn't much of a fight. One drunk eighteen-year-old, mourning the end of his youth, and of his oldest friendships, trying to make his rich uncle understand his pain.

Loedie's parting shot was half defiant, half defeated.

It's fine, he said. We'll see you in court.

For Marie, Loedie's younger sister, nothing would ever be quite the same again. She had grown up surrounded by this crowd of older boys. By Muller and the other 204s. She knew her cousin Muller had a temper and would never back down when the boys fought. But they were her world. More than brothers, more than family.

"They were blood," she said. Were.

But now that was all over, and she thought she understood why. Muller and his cousins had done something so wrong, so bad that they'd felt cornered. They'd realised that the only way out was to lie – to themselves, and to Muller's wealthy father, Oom Vicky, who was so rich and so good at fixing problems – and then to pin all the blame on her brother and father.

Marie shrugged. "So, yeah. It's taken care of," she said.

20

NOT GUILTY

HARVEST TIME HAD come around again. Pale gold fields and an early mist dissolving into clear skies. Ruth sat with her head against the car window, watching the landscape slipping past – a bristling rash of red flowers near the roadside, weaver bird nests hanging like baubles from a bare acacia tree, a group of clay-coloured impala grazing behind a fence on the inside slope of the crater.

Biltong, she said, as she eyed the antelope, giving her small gruff chuckle. Any excuse to think about something else today.

They'd all risen early for the first day of the trial. Ruth and Elias had walked out from the shack to the main road to wait for a lift, but Lawrence had decided to stay at home – his shoes had fallen apart and he felt he had nothing suitable to wear to court. Elias had put on a blue checked shirt and, while the sun was still at work on the morning chill, lent his leather jacket to his mother.

Ruth had a boyfriend now – someone from the abattoir in Sasolburg. Isaac. Nothing serious. I'm only playing, not marrying – I'm too old, she'd laugh. She was fifty-six and looking forward to retirement. Eish. What a strange life it had been. She thought of school, of setting off before five each morning to walk in the dark for two hours from her parents' house. That was far to the north west from here, towards Botswana, in the old black homeland of Bophuthatswana. Ruth had been good at school – number one in her class, a keen 400-metre runner, and good at choir too. There had even been a trip once, to sing in a competition in Pretoria, and to win a cup. But she was the youngest of eight children – four girls and four boys – and when her mother got sick and her father was away on the farms, she was the one told to stay home from school to look after her mother, which she did until her mother died. That was in 1981. Ruth was twenty years old by then and couldn't go back to school. Her father helped her to find work as a cleaner on a farm south of Parys. And then he got sick too – heart problems, and poor eyesight from all the welding work done without protection. And Ruth was married and a mother of three boys.

Now it was May 2017. Nearly a year and a half since Samuel and Simon had been killed. Ruth was both eager and scared to hear the details, to hear the truth spoken loudly and clearly. She'd quit her job and spoken to Captain Tshabalala about getting a lift in to Parys each day of the trial. At least the crowds outside the courthouse were gone now. Maybe that was because the local elections were finished. The E.F.F. had campaigned hard in Tumahole – Paul and his teams of red berets knocking on every shack and every door, holding their signs up at junctions, promising an end to the A.N.C.'s monopoly on local contracts, on jobs, on all the rest of it.

This is not a church council. We are here as fighters! Salut!

Salut!

Paul had been tough on his young volunteer army. It was the only way to get them organised.

It is a fact that you are all late. Let us not dispute that, he'd told a dozen of them, sternly, as a policewoman watched the group from across the street. In Tumahole, the E.F.F. leadership had plans to grab more government land, even though their last attempt had landed them in court and that case still hadn't come to any sort of resolution. The point was to keep making a noise. One of Paul's friends, a tall, thin, unremittingly cheerful playwright named Sandile, had written a special play ahead of the election. He'd called it "Life is War".

"Their anger is sleeping, but one day it will erupt."

Sandile would sometimes read out lines from memory.

"A flood is coming, and it will last for ever."

But when it had come to election day, the A.N.C. had still won more than 60 per cent of the vote across the Free State – a significant slide from the last ballot, but still enough to keep Paul and his colleagues out in the cold.

A few months after the election, the provincial government decided that Parys should have a flower festival, a grand parade through the centre of town, as part of a new campaign to promote the diversification of agriculture in the Free State. The route would be from the Steers restaurant, past the Cherry on Top, the police station, and down towards the Sasol garage. It was to be an annual event. Emissaries were dispatched to far-away Madeira to invite the island's participation. The result was a lively affair: perhaps a thousand people stood on the pavement to watch the Madeirans, in their straw hats and red peasant costumes, dance their way past the Pickled Pig pub, followed by men on stilts, several hundred local dancers, a beauty queen, and five extravagantly flower-garlanded floats. The provincial politicians who'd authorised the event drove the same route in half a dozen zebra-striped golf buggies, waving cheerfully. One of the officials had been having lunch, with her bodyguards, in an antique shop on Bree Street and had nearly missed the whole show.

In Tumahole, meanwhile, a nine-year-old girl playing with two friends in a muddy pit beside the unfenced rubbish dump, perhaps a hundred metres from Samuel's old shack, had drowned. Her death went unreported by any local media.

*

Simon's aunt, Selina, was already sitting on the wall outside the courthouse when Ruth and Elias arrived. One of Simon's younger sisters, Dimakatso, was there too, with her infant son strapped to her back in a light blue towel. They greeted each other. Selina showed Ruth an article about the trial in the local *Parys Gazette* – a paper that never reached Tumahole – where their two boys' surnames had been mixed up. Ruth shrugged. It wasn't the first time. They walked up the steps, through the broken metal-detector, and round to the right towards the smaller courtroom beyond the magistrate's office, where the six accused were already seated together in the dock. Their families occupied the bench immediately behind them, and the second bench was nearly full too – a long wooden seat, enough for fifteen people at a squeeze, with the beige wall behind it bruised by a dozen dark blotches, like grimy halos, where dozing heads had left their marks.

"Please speak up a bit, I'm a little hard of hearing. Sometimes I hear what I shouldn't hear ..."

Advocate Hans de Bruin stood at the lectern, bent-backed in a black gown with his left arm folded behind his back, and spoke in an ironic, almost chuckling tone – an old man accustomed to being indulged by younger members of the court, even by the judge. He was eighty years old and retired, but the defence team had begged him to represent the six accused at trial. Kobus Burger had assured them there was no-one like De Bruin when it came to cross-examinations.

He's a legend. His age is irrelevant. You'll see.

Seated behind De Bruin, Captain Prinsloo had already begun scribbling in a notebook. He was stuck now. Accused number 3. Sharing the same legal team, the same advocate, the same bench as the farmers. It was the only option he could afford. He'd already re-mortgaged his house and reckoned he was on his way to running up a quarter of a million rand in legal fees. Still, he was putting on his usual cheery face, joking – before the judge arrived – with the three youngsters to his left, trying to make light of things. Prinsloo had told his own family not to come to court. He couldn't cope with the extra stress, and nor, he felt, could they. His older daughter, Alicia, had struggled at her exams, missing all her targets and abandoning her plans to study dentistry. Yesterday afternoon, the younger girl, Arne, had had some sort of panic attack on the netball court.

And now it was time for Prinsloo to stand up, beside the others – a solitary, smart figure in his blazer, beside the checked shirts and unfamiliar ties of the farmers – to enter his plea.

"Not guilty."

Times six.

Boeta, then Anton, then the policeman, then Anton's boy Cor, who was now sporting a thin moustache, then Klein Loedie, and then his new brother-in-law, Miela. Miela and Crista had been planning to get married anyway at some point. But then their lawyers warned them that the prosecution might want Crista to give evidence at the trial. If they were man and wife, she couldn't be compelled to do so. They'd had a lovely wedding in Parys in March. Rikki had taken unpaid leave from her job at the epilepsy charity in town soon afterwards. Now she sat just behind her son and son-in-law, with a bag full of sandwiches at her feet.

Anton's wife, Gusta, sat beside her. You look nice, she told Rikki during a break.

Thanks, Rikki said, with a narrow smile.

In the dock the three younger accused seemed unsettled by the attention focused on them. The cameras, the whole business. They smirked and swaggered and tried to project a toughness which suited none of them and convinced no-one. The farmers among them had been working flat out with the harvest – a good one, at last – but the trial could not have begun at a worse time. They would be back out in the fields as soon as court was adjourned for the day. And now they also had to help Oom Loedie on his farm, even more than usual. Oom Loedie had not been the same since the incident.

He still refused to move out of his home, but he couldn't look after the cattle, and his heart was playing up. Clogged arteries. And he'd had a fall.

*

"There. Go forward! We sit here."

There was a sudden surge of tension on the front bench of the public gallery. A black man was trying to push his way towards Rikki and Gusta, to sit between them, and to bring his friends along to disrupt the unbroken line of white faces occupying the prime seats. The man was unemployed, a little drunk, and a familiar figure around court. He'd attended some of the bail hearings and, with his loud voice and brusque manner, seemed to channel the otherwise unspoken frustrations of those who squeezed onto the second bench, sometimes taking it in turns, sometimes stepping out of the courtroom to ensure that Ruth, Selina and the other relatives of the two dead men had somewhere to sit.

Rikki shuffled closer to the far wall, elbows clamped to her sides, her bag between her feet.

It was impossible.

*

The prosecution's first witness was a young, angular white man with close-cropped hair. Sergeant Gerhardus Keiser had been stationed at the police station in Parys since 2002 and had just come on duty at 6.00 p.m. on January 6, 2016 when a call came in from a private security company in town about a farm attack.

Keiser and a colleague had driven out to Bulrush farm and found Mr Loedewicus van der Westhuizen inside his house. He'd seemed calm, had even offered the policemen a cup of coffee, and no, he didn't want medical attention, he'd been firm about that. Keiser had taken a statement from the old man, and had then driven on to find Captain Prinsloo, getting lost on the way, and only reaching the scene of the incident after dark.

Prinsloo had shone his torch at the two bodies in the back of the pickup. Two African males. They were both unconscious; one of them had a swollen head, and there was a little blood on them, but not much.

"I told the captain that these people's injuries looked very, very serious and we should get medical help immediately," Keiser said.

"Then what?" state prosecutor J.J. Mlotshwa asked.

Each time before he asked a question, Mlotshwa would pause and cast a deferential glance towards the judge, who was taking hand-written notes of the proceedings.

Keiser explained how he'd called for an ambulance and arranged to rendezvous with it on the road somewhere between the field and Parys. As he described how the police had, carefully, transferred Simon and Samuel's bruised bodies from the white pickup to the back of their police van and how they had, gently, placed them on the metal floor, side by side, in the dock Anton's shoulders began to twitch.

Bullshit, he muttered under his breath. He'd seen what the police had really done. He had told Gusta as much that same evening when he'd finally got home. The cops had just thrown the two blacks into the van, head first. Like pieces of meat. Thank God I did nothing, he'd said to his wife.

"Did you say thirty-four kilometres?" asked De Bruin, beginning his cross-examination a few minutes later. A sceptical smile played on his lips. How could the police make such a basic mistake about the distance between Bulrush farm and the field where the men had been arrested?

"I said three or four kilometres," replied the policeman in the witness box.

Ohforfucksake. Captain Laux, seated with his Hawks colleagues just behind the prosecution, sighed, swore quietly, rolled his eyes and looked around the courtroom. He thought De Bruin was hopeless.

But over the course of the next few days, and the next few witnesses, the defence began to reveal something of its strategy. It had started with Keiser's observation that there was "not much blood" on either of the injured men at the scene, moved on to the corrugated sheet metal in the back of the police van the two men had been put into – a van that had quickly been cleaned out after the event – and then focused on a series of deep head wounds that two local paramedics, dispatched with their ambulance, had noticed on Simon and Samuel.

"One had a deep laceration at the back of his head," said paramedic David Mongali. "One of them … was bleeding a lot."

Relebone Marosela, another emergency medic, confirmed this. "They'd bled a lot, My Lady," she said. She had driven out in her own emergency vehicle and caught up with the ambulance as it was pulling over beside the police van. "I tried to stop the bleeding using bandages. It was still bleeding a lot. The wound was approximately one centimetre deep, in the middle of the back of the head, going downwards. The other victim had a wound below his chin, maybe half a centimetre deep," she said. The paramedics had secured neck collars around both men and lifted them onto flat trauma boards.

It was at this point in the proceedings that Ruth stood up, shuffled her way along the back row, and left quietly through the side door. A few minutes later, during a court break, Selina joined her outside.

Df-df-df-df-df-df-df … said Ruth, her hand on her chest, indicating how fast her heart was beating.

Then they sat quietly together, not talking.

By the time they went back inside after the break, De Bruin was already on his feet, busy confirming that the paramedics had seen no cushions in the back of the police van.

No "nice mattresses" either? he said.

No.

The implication was becoming clear. The defence planned to argue that Samuel and Simon had left the scene in poor shape, certainly, and with bruises, and some swelling, but with no obvious cuts or bleeding. And yet, by the time they'd met up with the ambulance, perhaps seven kilometres away from the field, their condition had changed dramatically, and perhaps fatally.

Later, after the court had adjourned and the accused were all milling around in the courtyard, waiting to drive home, Kobus Burger spelled it out.

"Something must have happened to them. Something immense," he said. And that something was the track that linked the dirt road with the corner of the field where the men had been assaulted. The track was so bad there it was almost impassable. It had broken the suspension on Wicus' car. Now imagine two injured men lying unsecured on a corrugated-iron floor in the back of a police van, being thrown around, violently, unable to protect themselves from further injury.

"Take my word for it. In our law, it's called novus actus interveniens," Burger declared, a chuckle bubbling up from his chest. Something new had emerged, an unforeseeable incident that broke the causal connection between the crime and subsequent events. It was so simple, and the prosecution had been the one to open the gates. The defence didn't have to lift a finger.

"I'm going to get fucking drunk," Burger announced. "We've earned it."

21

SOMETHING UNSEEN

THE GOVERNMENT MORTUARY in Bloemfontein is the largest in the country. It is a low-rise brick complex recently built beside a railway line in the city centre, with industrial-style loading bays, light-filled office facilities, an abundance of gleaming metal surfaces, and a hangar-like central space with two rows of fixed tables for post-mortems.

On the morning of January 13, 2016, Doctor Buang Lairi, a short man with a half-hearted moustache, who'd recently sold his private medical practice and was now battling to complete his forensic pathology degree, prepared to examine the refrigerated bodies of two unidentified black males.

The first body had been brought to Bloemfontein from Sasolburg and was simply labelled S.D.R. 18/2016. Dr Lairi immediately noticed scrapes and abrasions on the chest and abdomen, extensive bruising on the back, and what was known in the townships as "blue eyes" – pronounced black bruising around both eyes, better known in medical circles as raccoon-eyes. The raccoon, Dr Lairi would later inform the judge in Parys, in his measured, conscientious manner, "is a small, cat-like wild animal, grey but black around the eyes".

Dr Lairi noted that S.D.R. 18/2016 was 1.65 centimetres tall, weighed 63.9 kilograms, was of average physique and had no special identifying features such as tattoos or scars. As he worked his way around the body, the doctor observed that three ribs were broken on each side, that there was significant bleeding inside the lining of the heart and around both kidneys, and, most serious of all, that there was blood inside the skull, in the pro-tective lining of the brain, and inside the brain matter itself.

The second body – B.D.R. 35/2016 – belonged to a slightly taller man, who weighed five kilograms more than S.D.R. 18/2016. He also had no special identifying features. Dr Lairi estimated his age as thirty-seven. This body had arrived from Bloemfontein's Pelonomi Hospital, just a short drive across town, and it still bore the marks of emergency medical intervention and intubation – an air-tube down his throat, an intravenous drip and so on. This man's face appeared more swollen than his friend's, but he didn't have raccoon-eyes. He had abrasions on his forehead, a gash below his left eye, and another wound behind his left ear. There was bruising elsewhere, but not all of it easy to spot, given his dark skin. As with S.D.R. 18/2016, there was also evidence of substantial bleeding inside the skull and of serious harm to the brain itself.

In both cases, Dr Lairi concluded that the cause of death was multiple injuries – that the men had received numerous injuries that could, independently or together, have proved fatal – but that the mechanism of death – the "final insult", as he would later put it – was brain damage.

Both men had received such heavy blows to the head that severe swelling had occurred inside their skulls, and the only way for the pressure to be released was through the hole at the base of the skull – the foramen magnum – where the spinal cord runs. When the brain matter began pushing against that hole it also compressed the cord, cutting off key instructions from the brain to the rest of the body, above all to the heart and lungs. Death followed soon afterwards.

*

Sixteen months after performing the post-mortems, having just turned fifty and still without his forensic pathology degree, Dr Lairi drove to court in Parys, carrying with him the findings of his examinations and a steady confidence in his conclusions. He'd known, of course, something about the farm attack before he'd examined Simon and Samuel's bodies. It had been all over the news, and besides, it was good practice to find out as much as possible about each case beforehand, so you could have some sort of idea about what you should be looking for when it came to opening someone up on the table. Dr Lairi prided himself on being professional and leaving his emotions at home, but sometimes it was hard.

A few days before Dr Lairi was due to testify, he'd been watching the news on television and had seen a report from Coligny, a tiny farming town north-west of Parys. The place was on fire. Riots, street battles with the police, looting, an armoured police car, a tractor, trucks, dozens of small shops, and several farms and homes set alight by furious crowds. The protests had begun soon after the death of a sixteen-year-old boy, who'd been caught by two white workers on the farm stealing sunflower seeds from one of their fields. The two men insisted the boy had jumped out of the back of their bakkie as they were transporting him to the police station in town and had broken his neck. But a witness surfaced, insisting that he'd seen the boy being thrown from the van and beaten to death by the men. The authorities were still investigating the incident when senior A.N.C. politicians addressed the funeral rally and told the crowds that there was no confusion about the case – this was a race crime and white South Africans needed to understand that they were all "visitors in this country".

On Monday, May 8, the local magistrate in Coligny granted the two white men bail. More rioting followed.

It was four days after that that Dr Lairi arrived at court in Parys. In his opinion the two cases were linked. South Africa, he sometimes told his friends, was only a "so-called democracy". Blacks had no power.

Kobus Burger, standing in the sunshine outside court, had his own view on the Coligny case and expressed it in his trademark manner – "Bullshit! A cooked-up pot of nonsense." In fact, the magistrate in Coligny was a friend of his and hats off to him for giving bail to those two. Like everyone else, Burger had heard the provincial A.N.C. leadership's comments at the boy's funeral. It was indeed just like the Parys case, but only in the sense that politicians were, as usual, trying to whip up racial hatred in order to deflect attention from their own spectacular failings. The A.N.C. never bothered to visit white farmers who'd been attacked. Sure, the boy might have been hungry, but that didn't mean he should steal. What if Burger wanted to walk into a shop and take something to eat without paying? It was going to be chaos.

*

Ruth and Selina sat together in the back row in the courtroom, initially trying to crane their necks to catch a glimpse of a thick folder of pictures taken by a police photographer during the post-mortems, which Dr Lairi was now discussing with the judge and prosecutor.

"The raccoon-eyes show nicely on that one," Dr Lairi said, leafing breezily through the file. "You can see there, that's a blunt trauma to the back of the head. The deceased was most likely pulled along the ground as he was facing down. The English call that 'gravel-rash'. And here, in photo number twenty, there's a clot around the other kidney."

Before he'd even reached his conclusion – that this was a "very vicious assault" – Ruth had heard enough. She stood up and made her way outside, took a big drink of water from the tap in the far corner, and sat in her usual spot in the shade, to the left of the front entrance, to wait for Selina to come out during the next break.

I can't hear about the skull and the brain. My heart attack will start again, Ruth told her. She seemed to approach her own health in the same ruggedly down-to-earth spirit that she tackled cleaning jobs – gamely diagnosing various ailments and consuming large quantities of water and aspirins to combat high blood pressure and sore kidneys.

That one with the injury to the back is Simon, Selina said.

No, they were talking about my son, Ruth replied. That was Samuel.

A long pause followed as the two women watched the prosecution team walk past with the Hawks, trailing a broken cloud of cigarette smoke behind them.

His upper jaw was broken.

My son also had his jaw broken.

My boy's ribs are broken.

The one with no eyes is Simon.

It was not an argument. There was no tension, no competitiveness in Ruth and Selina's disagreement. There was simply confusion, and the intense desire for there to be no confusion; for them to be sure that the injuries, the gruesome descriptions they'd been listening to so attentively all morning, had belonged to their own flesh and blood, and were finally being properly acknowledged in court.

The source of the confusion lay not with the women themselves, nor with their faltering command of English – in court a translator was carefully explaining each detail in Sesotho – but rather with a legal system, and a particular trial, that seemed to attach little importance to the individual identities of the deceased. It was as though Simon and Samuel's dead bodies had been, rhetorically, blended into one conveniently ambiguous piece of flesh.

I can't tell you which deceased, but one, or both, was lifted high from the ground and thrown down, said one lawyer.

I can't remember now which one.

I think it was the shorter one.

Is that the taller suspect?

One of the suspects was wearing a blue jacket but I can't tell which one.

For days on end, the prosecution and defence both seemed to wallow in the confusion, unwilling or unable to distinguish between Simon and Samuel.

"I didn't think it was necessary to differentiate," Advocate de Bruin finally admitted, in a tetchy flash of honesty.

Dr Lairi displayed little inclination to set them right. Even the judge, a soft-spoken, seemingly amiable white woman called Corne van Zyl, showed no great appetite to resolve the matter.

"I can't make it out … I don't think we should make a definite determination of the identity at this stage," she said, peering at two photographs which clearly showed Samuel slumped in the bakkie and then lying on a hospital bed.

*

The cross-examination of Dr Lairi began gently. The elderly defence advocate, De Bruin, left hand still clenched behind his back, spoke of the need for mutual respect and honesty, and for an early acknowledgement that forensic pathology was not a very exact science.

"Never and always. Two words that are never used," De Bruin proposed.

"Seldom say never, seldom say always," Lairi countered with a smile.

The defence was sticking to its strategy. First came the suggestion that one of the deceased – as usual, there was no attempt to be specific – might have broken his ribs when he was tackled to the ground during his arrest, and not by any of the accused.

Lairi conceded that was possible.

Perhaps the broken ribs alone could have killed him?

Lairi felt that was unlikely.

De Bruin took the doctor through each of the various assaults alleged to have been carried out by the accused. The gun, the stick, the Taser/cattle-prod, the knife, the monkey-wrench, and Anton's large shoes.

"You'll agree that he is an exceptionally big man," De Bruin said, asking Anton Loggenberg to stand up in the dock.

The judge agreed he was.

"Are you really wanting to tell me that if you put 195 kilos of human, trampling, on the head of a man, you will not find a trace – not a trace – on the cheeks or head, or anywhere?" De Bruin asked Dr Lairi.

"If he stood on him with both feet I would expect to see something," Lairi agreed. But he wondered if accused number 2 had perhaps used one leg for balance. "One might have no injuries outside, but inside we see the damage," he said.

In the dock, Anton folded his arms over his chest and stared straight ahead.

Next, Dr Lairi was asked about Cor Loggenberg's alleged use of a stick, a kierie, to beat one of the men on the shins.

No, he'd not seen any marks to indicate that.

The same went for Loedie's alleged assault with the monkey-wrench.

"A hit with this would surely have fractured the skull," De Bruin said, theatrically failing to lift the heavy wrench from the table.

"I agree," Lairi said.

As for Captain Prinsloo and the Taser – no, Lairi had not found any burns or other signs of possible electrocution on the groin areas, or anywhere else, on either of the bodies.

"I didn't see anything, but that doesn't mean it did not happen. Sometimes we see wounds. Sometimes we don't," Lairi said.

"I'm going to argue that you're vague – that you're trying to argue anything that goes against you," De Bruin shot back.

The defence advocate then turned to the issue of the gun Boeta van der Westhuizen had allegedly used to beat Simon on the head. The gun was small enough to fit into a woman's handbag, he said. Were the cuts on Simon's face consistent with being beaten unconscious with the butt of the revolver?

"It's difficult to ascribe any injury on the body to that specific gun," Lairi conceded. Then, getting confused between the two bodies again, he said, "I can't remember which one … there is one who had a suture below the left eye."

But even then, he admitted, the wound was too small. If Boeta had really smashed him in the face with the gun, then the wound and the bone damage would have been more extensive.

"You said this was a vicious assault – you said that?"

"I did."

"So, where's the viciousness?" De Bruin asked, with a triumphant smile.

*

Dr Lairi was asked about the anthill incident – the claim that Muller van der Westhuizen, who was now a state witness, had picked up one of the men and repeatedly hurled him, like a wrestler, onto the rocky ground. "Fucked him up ... threw him down on an anthill and shit like that," as Muller had boasted on WhatsApp.

Would the doctor concede that the fractured ribs, the injuries to one of the deceased's kidneys, the blunt trauma that could be linked to the head injuries, all of this could be the result of that kind of assault?

"If I knew which of the deceased it was, I would be able to say more,' Lairi said, but yes, the bruises, the cuts, the clots, and the blunt force trauma could have caused those injuries.

The defence returned to their key argument: that both men could have sustained fatal injuries on the drive from the scene in the back of the police van to where they had met up with the ambulance.

This line of enquiry, De Bruin argued, was of the utmost importance for the case.

In order to see the terrain, the road, to experience the driving conditions, the defence asked the court for an inspection "in loco".

"We'd like the doctor to be present," he said.

The judge agreed, and the following morning she, the prosecution, the defence, the accused, the Hawks and some accompanying policemen drove out, first to Oom Loedie's Bulrush farm, and then to the dry field where Simon and Samuel had been caught and assaulted.

So it's a rough veld area with stones, said the judge, walking through the dry grass.

Kobus Burger pointed out the two water tanks where, he was convinced, the gun used to attack the old white farmer had been thrown. They looked at the nearby fence, and the line of trees behind it, and then returned to the convoy of vehicles to follow the path that the police van had taken that night as it drove Simon and Samuel away.

"It was terrible," Advocate de Bruin declared in court a couple of hours later. "The vehicle was driven over the worst terrain I've ever seen."

"It was rough terrain. Not a stable ride," Lairi conceded. Still, he hadn't observed anyone in his car clinging onto anything for balance.

De Bruin pointed out that the two men in question had been unconscious. They would have been unable to stabilise themselves as the police van lurched up and down through ditches. They would have been thrown up and down against the sharp metal edges of the side benches and floor.

"They roll, and they bob, and they bang their heads … bobbing up and down …"

"My Lady, I would imagine for that to happen they would have had to be travelling at very high speed," said Dr Lairi.

"I'm going to argue to Her Ladyship that you are intendedly trying to shy away from the possibility – the probability – that those guys were seriously injured in the back of that van," De Bruin said sternly.

And what was more, the doctor had missed a key piece of evidence in his post-mortem.

"You missed it!" De Bruin cried.

He was referring to the vertical wound, five centimetres long and one centimetre deep, that the paramedic had noticed on the back of one of the men's heads. The wound that had been bleeding profusely as he was transferred from the police van to the ambulance.

"Red blood. Profuse bleeding."

De Bruin wanted Lairi to admit that this was proof of a fresh wound, in which case it would surely have been sustained in the back of the police van, not before. "Would you comment, or rather stay quiet?" he asked.

The truth was that Dr Lairi had, indeed, failed to spot the wound during the autopsy.

"Why did you miss it?"

"Perhaps it had been stitched up," he ventured apologetically. "If it's sutured under the skin it is difficult to see. But it is difficult to understand why. I don't know."

After several hours standing in the witness box, the doctor was struggling, his smile gone, his usual affability exhausted.

Had the police mentioned seeing lots of blood beforehand? he enquired.

No, was De Bruin's reply.

"In that case I would say most likely he got the cut during that rough ride," Lairi said.

"And if a man can sustain such an exterior wound on his head, why not an interior one, in the brain, in the skull? Why not?"

"That is possible," Lairi conceded.

But the humiliation of being challenged by this elderly man, picked apart, his dignity questioned, his professionalism undermined, had unlocked something in Dr Lairi, something he knew he was not supposed to reveal in court.

"Can I ..." Lairi paused, then turned away from the

judge towards the rest of the courtroom. "I think this honour-able court will know the example of the late Steve Biko," he began.

A ripple of something unseen shivered around the room, or parts of it. Hairs prickled on the backs of necks. J.J. Mlotshwa looked up sharply from the prosecution desk. The back bench of the public gallery creaked, quietly, as bodies shifted as if moving to accommodate an unexpected presence.

Afterwards, in the sunshine outside, Dr Buang Lairi would reach for boxing metaphors to describe his behaviour. He'd felt cornered, had felt as though he was being hit below the belt, and wanted to punch back in the most powerful way he could, by making an explicit link between the tactics of a group of white lawyers defending six white men and one of the most notorious crimes of the old apartheid state.

De Bruin had tried to cut him off.

"You're trying to shy away from questions and using examples that are not applicable to this case — at all," he protested.

But Lairi would not be stopped. "Biko was taken in the back of a bakkie, after being assaulted by special forces, from Port Elizabeth to Pretoria ... and he was just thrown into the cell that night, and the next morning the state pathologist said his cause of death was suicide. I want to state this categorically. If I get a head injury that leaves me unconscious, the person who killed me is the one who made me unconscious." It was the beating that mattered. Anything else, anything that might have happened in the back of a police van on a dirt road, he said, was immaterial.

"Steve Biko travelled on a tarred road. Not so?" De Bruin calmly interjected.

"I don't know."

"You're avoiding the issue that a person on a corrugated floor will get bruises, and an aggravated brain injury."

"No. I don't think so. Not in my opinion." Lairi noted that Biko had been driven hundreds of kilometres, and that the police van transporting Samuel and Simon had travelled perhaps a kilometre or less over the field before joining the dirt road for another few kilometres. "Eleven kilometres is not a long distance. That is my candid opinion," he concluded.

The judge finally intervened. This was a legal argument, she said. She spoke gently, diplomatically, but her meaning was clear: a doctor, brought here to discuss a post-mortem, should not be speculating about politics and history.

Before he was dismissed as a witness, Dr Lairi was briefly questioned once more by the prosecution. Did he agree that, at the speed the police van had been travelling, further injuries were unlikely?

At that speed, honestly, he wouldn't expect more injuries.

And what about the cut on B.D.R. 35/2016's face – could it have been caused by a blow from a firearm?

Yes, it could.

Lairi's smile returned as he left the courthouse and walked across the road to his car. He knew he shouldn't have said all that about Biko. After all, he was not a politician. But he could see he'd touched a raw nerve.

"Oh, that was nonsense," was Kobus Burger's opinion afterwards. "Biko was transported on a tarred road. You see what happens with this doctor. Every time he's basically forced to make a concession he tries to cover it up. Now he brings this Steve Biko thing along. It has nothing to do with that." As for the post-mortem itself, Burger still had more questions. It wasn't just one wound that Dr Lairi had overlooked. Burger had seen the evidence of another doctor in Bloemfontein, from the man who'd first received Simon's body. That doctor had noted a large skull fracture, he could feel a crack in the bone from the forehead back towards the top of the head. How could Lairi have missed that? Maybe the truth was that they'd got the bodies mixed up – had done the post-mortem on someone entirely different. Not Simon.

"I don't know who that person was, but it couldn't have been him," Burger declared.

It sounded far-fetched. But then again, this case was littered with mistakes. Even the Hawks' own docket was wrong – it had photographs of Samuel and Simon's bodies, taken by a farmer when they were in the bakkie. Just like the *Parys Gazette*, and multiple prosecution documents, the Hawks had got their names the wrong way round.

22

LIKE A MOSQUITO BITE

THE TRIAL, WHICH began in May 2017, was scheduled to last a month. It soon became clear that that was wildly optimistic.

Early on, there were long delays for arguments about evidence, about access to the trove of WhatsApp messages, and about a last-minute appeal by the S.A.B.C. to film and broadcast the proceedings live. Then, as the prosecution finally moved away from the more forensic aspects of its case and began calling witnesses to testify about exactly who had done what to whom, the professional courtesies and mutual respect which had, to some extent, survived the early skirmishes between the opposing lawyers in court, began to collapse.

"I'm not going to take that lying down," state prosecutor J.J. Mlotshwa spat out one morning, riled once too often by Kobus Burger's habitual sarcasm.

"They're as crooked as the police," Burger whispered in the corridor. "They came to court and lied. They lied in the judge's face."

He was talking about the damaging allegation about him, that he'd urged his clients to burn their evidence and erase everything on their mobiles. The issue had now been raised in court, without warning, by the state. It was a matter that could jeopardise Burger's career.

"It's bullshit," he grumbled. It was another cynical attempt to disrupt and distract.

But in private the defence team appeared worried – about the prosecution's tactics, about the delays, and about the judge too. Could she keep order? Would she let Mlotshwa run riot and waste time? Nico Dreyer, an experienced Bloemfontein criminal advocate, who had been assisting De Bruin, said he liked this judge, respected her, but these days South African judges – especially the white ones – were wary about how they dealt with the state, afraid they'd be accused of bias, and as a result didn't intervene nearly as much as they should. Look what the prosecution had already done to Magistrate Pillay. There was a pattern. And now, Dreyer worried, the prosecution was playing games – tit-for-tatting – whenever they got shown up or embarrassed in court.

*

On the morning of May 17, 2017, the day after Dr Lairi had finished giving evidence, Ockert van Zyl took off his black cowboy hat, stubbed out a cigarette, swaggered into court in a red shirt and black jacket, and took his place in the witness box. Van Zyl – part-time farmer, perfume-packager, friend of accused number 2, Anton Loggenberg, and the man who'd boasted of killing "two kaffirs" – repeated the allegations he'd already told Captain Laux and the Hawks. How he'd arrived at the scene to find two black men lying in Anton's bakkie, one of them seemingly dead, the other being whipped with a fan-belt by accused number 1, Boeta van der Westhuizen, and shocked in his groin by accused number 3, Captain Prinsloo. The victim was coughing and spitting up blood but wasn't conscious enough to try to block the assault. Boeta and the policeman were joking around with the Taser. Van Zyl was worried he'd get covered in blood.

"It was," he said, savouring his catchphrases, "no tea party. It was wild there, like dogs hunting a hare."

But no, he hadn't see his friend Anton, nor Anton's son Cor, doing anything wrong, and yes, he was ashamed of the words he'd spoken the following morning to the manager at the carwash. He couldn't explain why he'd boasted about killing anyone.

Under cross-examination the following day, Van Zyl stuck to his version. There was a long but inconclusive argument about the difference between whipping and tapping someone on the face. The defence secured a small but significant victory when Van Zyl acknowledged that he had not heard the trademark clicking noise that a shocking device usually emits when it is fully charged and used.

But still, Van Zyl insisted, it was no tea party. "It was a beating. If that was done to me, I would have regarded it as a beating."

*

The following Saturday evening, drunk and angry, Anton Loggenberg called Ockert van Zyl on his mobile from his pickup. He was driving on a farm road after a day out hunting with some other farmers.

"Howzit, my friend, blah blah blah ..."

Ockert could hear the whisky talking as Anton began to rant about the case, about the Hawks, about the treacherous 204 state witnesses who were now beginning to testify, about what he'd say to them all, right now, if only they could hear him.

"I wish the idiots would be listening now. Because I'm going to get rid of them. I'm going to shoot them. The joiners will all be shot dead."

"Joiners" is a powerful word in Afrikaans. It refers to those Afrikaners who fought with the British during the Anglo-Boer War. The worst sort of traitors. And here was Anton using the same word today to conjure up some kind of all-or-nothing battle against those now siding with the South African state and against their own kin.

That was how Ockert remembered the phone call.

Anton had a very different memory of their conversation that evening. Yes, he'd been driving – near Ockert's farm, in fact – and yes, he'd been in a bad mood. But he was angry because he suspected that his friend was cheating him, was taking advantage of the distraction of the trial and the fact that the two men were not, by law, supposed to be in communication for its duration, to squeeze Anton out of his share of the profits from a cattle deal.

For a while now, Anton had been looking after some of Ockert's cattle – injecting them, burning the horns, running the whole place like it was his – initially in return for cash, but more recently on the understanding that he would earn 20 per cent of the value of any calves sold. That evening, after hearing a rumour that Ockert was putting his whole farm on the market, he'd driven over to the field to check on the cattle and found that the gate was newly padlocked.

So he'd got Ockert on the telephone to ask him what the hell was going on.

That was all.

*

The following Tuesday, Anton learned, with some surprise, that he was being charged with intimidation. The state was going to request that the court revoke his bail and send him back to prison for the duration of the trial.

Just like what had happened with Boeta.

It was because, as Captain Laux explained it, Mr van Zyl had telephoned him at the weekend in a panic. Mr van Zyl was convinced that his friend's drunken threats — towards the joiners, and perhaps towards him too — were serious.

"Mr van Zyl is feeling very threatened and afraid for his life," Laux said to the courtroom. "He said to me that if something happens to the joiners, he doesn't want it on his hands."

Kobus Burger rose from his seat to cross-examine the captain, his voice and demeanour heavy with contempt and scepticism. "The timing is quite peculiar," he began. "Which is a nicer word for strange."

He then went on to outline his client's version of events: the plot that Van Zyl was obviously hatching against his friend to sell the cattle and keep his share. "And wouldn't that be a nice way to get rid of Anton and his interest in the cows – to get him locked up in jail? A nice move," he said with a smile.

There was more to it than that though. This wasn't just about two friends falling out over money. Burger couldn't spell it out in court, but he suspected that the prosecution was using the incident to punish the defence. A few days earlier, the defence had made a big deal in court about alleged corruption by the Hawks – bringing up the claims that Laux and Topkin had threatened and beaten witnesses. It had been humiliating for the prosecution and now the prosecution was looking for revenge. Tit-for-tatting.

But if that was the case, Captain Laux was not part of it. Summoned to the witness box to give evidence against Anton, he looked red-faced and sour. He'd already told his colleagues they were making a mistake by trying to revoke Anton's bail – it wasn't going to work and it could get complicated. But they'd insisted and so now he was being put on the spot.

The truth – which Laux was trying to hide – was that the Hawks knew about Anton's call, not because Ockert van Zyl had told them about it but because they'd been tapping accused number 2's phone – were still tapping it, and plenty of others. They had a recording of the entire six-and-a-half-minute conversation. It was a secret the Hawks didn't want revealed in court.

Eventually, after three precious and expensive days of court time, Van Zyl's claim was dismissed – after all, he'd already admitted to lying when he'd boasted of killing two men – and the state was overruled regarding bail. Anton Loggenberg remained a free man for now.

Van Zyl promptly left town, returning to his home north of the crater's edge. A few days later, in a restaurant in Klerksdorp, he reflected on his experience with a visitor. To the question, "What would happen if he returned to Parys?", Van Zyl ran one of his long fingers across his throat. And what of his friendship with Anton? He raised a middle finger. He was given to hand gestures as well as catchphrases.

"Anton knows what he did that night," Van Zyl said, referring to the incident in the field, "which I'm not prepared to say. I did not mention it in my statement. It was never mentioned. But he knows."

*

After that scrap, the mood in court became even more hostile. The defence team shook their heads, rolled their eyes, and said they'd never experienced anything like it. Captain Prinsloo downloaded an app that claimed to be able to detect electronic bugs, and each morning he would waft it, conspicuously, around the defence lawyers' table and the dock.

Then Fanie Oosthuizen – the first of the 204s, the former miner turned farm foreman, who'd been charged with murder, had accused the Hawks of threatening him and his family, and had then embraced the opportunity to turn state witness – was called to give evidence.

He walked into the courtroom, a jowly figure in a short-sleeved checked shirt and dark tie, staring straight ahead, avoiding the withering stares of the men to his left. Whispers were aimed at him. Here he was, the first of the joiners to take the stand. The word "bodyguard" floated back to the public benches – something about how Fanie would be needing one now.

As he began to describe the events, the three younger accused, Cor, Loedie and Miela, exchanged smirks and glances, raising their eyebrows.

"They wouldn't listen to me," Fanie said to the judge, after the prosecutor asked why he hadn't stopped the young farmers' assault. "They just regard me as a farmworker."

Boeta and Anton glared straight ahead, but Cor Loggenberg sniggered loudly. He couldn't stop himself. Loedie and Miela tried not to join in, but soon all three of the boys had their hands over their mouths. The courtroom guard strode over from the wall, his finger in front of his mouth, silently ordering the youngsters to behave.

But the judge had noticed.

"We offer his apologies," said the defence advocate, De Bruin. Accused number 4 was, he suggested, "extremely upset about what he heard from the witness. He was crying. He was so upset he couldn't restrain himself."

"It seemed more like he was laughing at what he'd heard," the judge replied.

"It was more of a grimace than a smile," insisted De Bruin, with an ingratiating smile of his own.

*

Ruth was not in court that day. She'd taken the week off to get some cleaning done and to try to get electricity connected to her shack. The kerosene lamp was expensive and dirty, and she'd been borrowing too much money from her neighbours. Elias was there though. He sat in the back row beside Simon's aunt, Selina, who had also been asked to keep quiet by the guard because she couldn't help groaning, or sighing, when the witnesses spoke of "the shorter man". She'd decided, wrongly, that probably referred to Simon, but no-one seemed sure.

"The white people – see how they are in there," Elias complained during the next break. "It's like a mosquito bite, like they can just brush it all away. They're laughing. It makes my heart …" He looked away, embarrassed by his own emotions.

*

Fanie stuck carefully to his statement. Yes, the youngsters had assaulted both men that evening and so had he and his brother. All the 204s were guilty. But not of murder. A few punches, for sure. Arms twisted. One man dropped to the ground from waist height. But Simon and Samuel had both been fine, still sitting up, still able to talk, by the time they'd done with them.

"It was only slaps and kicks … nothing vicious."

And then Boeta and Anton had arrived.

It was De Bruin's turn to cross-examine Fanie. But today the elderly lawyer appeared to be struggling. He used the wrong names, complained of tiredness, frequently misunderstood the judge, asked about a hammer rather than a gun, and repeatedly seemed to veer off track.

"What is the ninth commandment?" he asked a bemused Fanie.

"I don't know."

"One of the canons of Christianity is to take care of your master ..."

Behind him, Boeta and Anton were frowning and passing notes forwards to their lawyers.

The next morning, the judge announced that the accused had sacked their advocate, and the trial would have to be postponed. The defence team explained that De Bruin had done a wonderful job but had experienced some sort of mild stroke a few days earlier. But as De Bruin left the courtroom, shuffling towards the exit and past the line of accused, he paused. He didn't mention his health. Instead he said, to Anton: "I wish you'd told me you weren't happy, rather than going behind my back."

Accused number 2 flushed but said nothing.

"I'm not mad at you," De Bruin said.

23

WHITE TERRORISTS

BY THE TIME the trial resumed, in November 2017, summer had returned, with sudden thunderstorms elbowing their way over the crater's rim.

Outside the Parys magistrate's court, two grey-haired men from the township, Ben and Sam, stood by the steps, soaking up the morning sun, hoping to get a good seat for the trial. They told a journalist that they were pastors and looking for new material for their Sunday sermons. They stepped back respectfully to make way for a young woman with a crying child on her back, who had come to get a protection order against her husband. Her husband had left her when she was pregnant but had since returned, with a new girlfriend, demanding full rights to the three-year-old girl, and beating her for refusing. "We see on television about child rapes. Even for three-year-olds," the mother explained in a whisper.

Further back from the steps, the usual groups had gathered in what were now their established corners. The state prosecutor, J.J. Mlotshwa, stood with his team in a huddle to the left of the front steps. He'd spent the intervening months training for one of his regular, sedately paced marathons, working on a complicated racketeering case involving Treasury officials, and trying to prosecute E.F.F. leader Julius Malema in relation to his calls for people to occupy land.

Behind him, under the trees, sat Ruth, wearing a blue patterned dress. She had lost weight. Her two remaining sons, Elias and Lawrence, were with her today. Selina, Simon's aunt, was there too and they all shared a bottle of soda, talking together in soft voices. Ruth had found a new job cleaning house for an ex-policeman, a white guy living near Heilbron, who paid her seventy rand a day. Selina wondered whether the trial would have dragged on this long if the dead men had been white.

A few yards away, across the steps that led down from the main road, Rikki van der Westhuizen sat quietly beside her husband Boeta. Kobus Burger spent a few moments mock-wrestling with Loedie and then went to greet the rest of the accused.

The 204s were keeping a lower profile these days, only turning up, individually and at the last minute, if, and when, they were required to testify.

Captain Francois Laux had retired. He had quit the case with a pronounced sense of relief – all that hatred directed at him online, people saying the Hawks were the bad guys, it would wear anyone down. While he was off exploring the country on his motorbike, his former Hawks colleagues, locked in a circle of leather jackets and cigarette smoke to the right of the courthouse, chatted about a sudden surge of cash-in-transit heists, seven in the Free State in the past month.

"They're killing us, these guys. They've got A.K.s, heavy weapons," one of Laux's old team grumbled.

At 9.00 a.m., Jeremia Tollie, the court translator, pitched up. He was a tall, genial 59-year-old who spoke eleven languages. He had just finished a trial in Harrismith involving six Zimbabweans and a Mozambican convicted of stealing copper cable.

Kobus Burger and the defence's new lead advocate, Nico Dreyer, were the last to arrive. Dreyer had to be helped out of Burger's car, which proved to be a delicate and strenuous operation, requiring all three of the young accused. Klein Loedie, Miela and Cor carefully transferred him from the low-slung car seat into a waiting wheelchair. Dreyer was reputed to be one of the best criminal defence lawyers in the province, maybe even the country, a straight-shooter who could usually count on the prosecution's respect. His health was poor and his weight had ballooned dangerously, to the extent that he could no longer walk more than a couple of steps unsupported.

"Eish," Rikki said, watching her son help roll his advocate backwards up the ramp beside the courthouse steps. "The poor man."

*

"Do you know accused number 1?" J.J. Mlotshwa began.

"Yes. He's my father's cousin."

"Accused number 2?"

"Yes, we grew up in the same area, with his children on the farms."

And on it went. As each of the young 204s – tanned, fair-haired, straight-backed cousins – took their turn in the witness box, the prosecutor methodically pinpointed their ties to the accused, who sat, staring hard at them, just a few feet away across the carpet. It was as if, by reminding the court of those ties, the state was hoping to emphasise the courage and the integrity of its witnesses – men who were prepared to betray their own relatives in order to speak the truth.

Accused number 4?

Yes, I know him. We were at school together.

He's my family.

He's Boeta's son.

He's a friend of my father's.

He's my relative.

He's a friend, married to my cousin.

We grew up together.

It felt like a sharp corner had been turned in the trial. Here was the family, finally, formally turning on itself. There was no way back for the Van der Westhuizens now.

First came Wicus van der Westhuizen, then Muller van der Westhuizen, and then Wian van der Westhuizen, each young man sworn in by the judge's clerk, and each warned, in turn, by the judge about the law regarding 204s: that if she concluded they'd been honest and open in their testimonies they would not be punished for any crimes in which they admitted taking part. If, on the other hand, they were deemed to be lying, then they would be in trouble.

The three cousins described the events of that evening in almost identical terms. Shepherded through their statements by Mlotshwa, they used similar phrases and painted similar pictures of each incident of violence. The gun. The kierie.

The monkey-wrench. The stamping. Their task was to stick to the state's case – that no serious, life-threatening violence against Simon or Samuel had occurred until those in the dock had got involved. Yes, the cousins were appropriately sorry for the punches and kicks they'd each thrown. But the right men were on trial.

Nico Dreyer's task was to expose this as a monstrous lie, to break the cousins, tear them to shreds, trip them up and tie them in knots. Between them, he and Burger would find the cracks in their well-polished versions and reveal how their accounts had been manipulated and edited to support the state's preposterous argument. Finally, Dreyer would force them to concede that they were as guilty as those in the dock and that the state's case was nothing more than a grubby deal that had enabled one half of a close-knit family to throw the other half to the wolves to avoid going to prison.

From his wheelchair, Dreyer was meticulous and relentless in his cross-examination.

First up was Wicus, by now a sturdy 21-year-old who wore his hair short. He had his sleeves rolled up his strong arms.

Almost immediately Dreyer asked the court for permission to play the WhatsApp voice messages on a small speaker that had been placed on the edge of the wooden witness box.

"We found the people! Two kaffirs. We found them!"

Something like a shudder rippled along the back bench.

"Is that your voice?" Dreyer asked Wicus.

"Yes."

Then Muller's notorious message was played – twice, for good measure.

"I fucked him up. I punched him in his stomach and in his ribs and kicked and damaged him. I threw him down on an anthill and shit like that. The police are here now and we told them the dogs fucked them up."

"I did not see that!" Wicus blurted out to the court, unprompted.

"You were there. How could you not have seen it?" Dreyer, his red face redder than usual, was almost snarling. "I put it to you that you're lying."

The defence would happily have kept replaying the WhatsApp messages all day. They were a powerful reminder of the 204s' murky moral footwork. But Mlotshwa objected, arguing that the court should not be forced to hear "the K-word", and more general swearing, more often than was strictly necessary.

"It's just not right, man. They're playing to the media," Colonel Topkin complained of the defence tactic. "It's not the word. It's the actions that count."

The judge agreed and asked Dreyer and Burger to be more selective in what they chose to play to the court.

*

The cross-examinations lasted days, with Dreyer, and sometimes Burger, hammering at the cousins.

"You're trying to minimise your actions."

"You tell lies when it suits you."

"Your statements are so similar. I put it to you that your version cannot be the truth!"

Over time, plenty of small discrepancies did emerge and were quickly seized on as part of a wider conspiracy. For the most part, though, the three young Van der Westhuizens managed to stick to their stories. Muller had only lifted one of the men to "hip height", "belt height", or "waist height" and then dropped him on the ground. Nothing fatal. Muller had obviously been boasting when he'd talked about it in that WhatsApp message. Whereas big Anton Loggenberg had definitely "stamped" or "trampled" on the man's head. Maybe they were uncertain about which foot he'd used, but nothing more. As for Boeta, there was no doubt. He'd used the revolver to hit "very hard, more than once", or "several times, to his forehead area", or "a few times". It was the same for Cor with the stick. And when the cousins' evidence seemed to contradict other witnesses, they would simply say something like: He saw what he saw. I saw what I saw.

The only significant confusion related to Loedie, accused number 5. Wian and Muller had seen him hit the ground beside the suspect's head with the monkey-wrench, whereas Wicus testified that Loedie had hit the side of the suspect's head.

And then there was the enduring question of which victim was Simon and which was Samuel. Sometimes the cousins talked about the taller man, or smaller man, or the lighter-skinned man; sometimes they referred to them by name, but there was no consistency, and no suggestion that anyone was absolutely sure who was who, or that it really mattered.

Still, there was no getting around the glaring fact of those WhatsApp messages. Muller's in particular, but also another one, from Wicus, in which he spoke of how the two victims were "already fucked up" early on, before Boeta or Anton had arrived at the scene.

"If a punch is going to kill you, then you know you were punched fucking hard!"

That voice message reflected the blame back towards the cousins, towards Fanie Oosthuizen and his son and brother; towards all those who'd arrived on the scene first and had already admitted to punching both men repeatedly.

But Wicus insisted that what the courtroom had heard him say in the WhatsApp voice recording was more boasting than real; it wasn't what had really happened. And he had been worried about that – that the WhatsApp message was being taken as telling the truth.

That was why he was here now, in court, under oath, to explain.

*

The trial was due to end on November 24, 2017. Thirty court days had already been used and, on more than one occasion, squandered, and the state still hadn't finished presenting its case. None of the accused had taken the stand yet.

Busy legal diaries were consulted, clerks' heads scratched, plans rearranged, bank loans extended, and three more weeks eventually located and reserved for almost six months ahead: the following May, 2018.

By then, well over two years would have passed since the killing of Simon Jubeba and Samuel Tjixa.

*

Out on the farms, between the rival Van der Westhuizens and their neighbours, a truce appeared to be holding, for the most part; each side trying to convince itself that, as events unfolded in court, the community's sympathies were shifting decisively in their direction. But as everyone understood, the truce was paper thin.

One evening Anton Loggenberg picked up his mobile and began typing furiously. His message was to the local farmers' security WhatsApp group.

"I have two murder cases against me and my son," he began. "The Weiveld Farmers Union immediately distanced themselves from what happened."

Then Anton got to his real point, which concerned the 204s and how he viewed their behaviour not just as a betrayal of their family and neighbours, but a betrayal of their race.

"We are sitting with WHITE TERRORISTS in our midst," he typed. "Wait until all the white people have nothing to lose and then maybe we'll have a chance ... Let's look after our white people first."

Overnight, and for a few hours into the next day, the WhatsApp group absorbed Anton's comments in silence, perhaps aware that, since the killings, such forums were no longer as private as they'd once been.

Then Fanie Oosthuizen couldn't resist a quick jab.

"The truth will be revealed. All the right people are being prosecuted. Take responsibility for yourself and don't be a coward," he typed.

Next came Kobus Dannhauser, head of the local farmers' union.

THESE ARE NOT GENTLE PEOPLE

"I've been wondering since last night if it is worth reacting to this rubbish," he began, before adding, pointedly, that "the person concerned was never a member of the farmers' association." "Let's get on with our work," he ended his message. "Have a good day."

Then more farmers began to weigh in. And none of them to support Anton.

"The reality is that every action has a reaction. If you don't think before you do something it can cost you dearly!"

"A true Afrikaner takes responsibility for what he has done, no matter how bad it might be, and sticks his neck out for his children."

"All I see is someone who is dodging and running out of options."

"Do to others as you would like them to do to you."

If Anton was disappointed by the reaction of his neighbours, he tried hard to hide it.

"It seems to me that I set the cat among the pigeons. WAKE UP PLEASE. We can only stand together if we don't stand against each other!!!!! Excuse me for what I've said but unfortunately it is the truth, and I'm stuck here with the lawyer's bill. I am deeply disappointed in my wonderful Weiveld farmers."

24

A LOW BUZZING NOISE

CAPTAIN HENK PRINSLOO stepped out of the shower, brushed his teeth, shaved, and then did something that had become a habit in recent months – he took his blood pressure. While the little machine did its thing, he looked in the mirror. He saw the round red face of a man fast approaching fifty, a man who had been kicked off his bowling team, had a new mortgage to contend with and a lawyer's bill that was now standing at over five hundred thousand rand. He'd thought this wretched trial might take a year but it was now May 2018, there was still no end in sight, and even if he was eventually cleared at trial the police service was planning its own disciplinary hearing.

When he heard the ping he looked down. His blood pressure was dangerously high: 185 over 120.

At least the girls were doing better now. He'd recently moved his family into a smaller, cheaper house out towards the cemetery, on a potholed road, half a dozen blocks west of the girls' school. Alicia had started a university degree in Potchefstroom, and Arne, with her guitar and her clear voice, had won in six separate categories of a nationwide talent contest. She had spent last weekend with friends, mucking around in fancy dress at the traffic lights on Bree Street, raising money for an air ticket to New York for the American version of the competition.

So it wasn't all bad, Prinsloo told himself.

In fact, on fine winter days like this, in the afterglow of a good harvest and the annual rugby week, Parys still felt like an optimistic place; not like so many of those inert, half-deserted farming towns which seemed to have had the life relentlessly sucked out of them for the past two decades. Coligny, for example. At least in Parys the municipality's audits were slowly emerging from the darkness – so what if the district owed Eskom almost a billion rand and the Free State authorities were sinking in a swamp of corruption. A new recreation centre had just opened in Tumahole. The second flower festival had taken place and it had been a bigger success than the first. And the tourists kept coming to the riverbanks.

Other changes had happened over the past few months. Magistrate Pillay had quit her job – for the sake of her sanity, she told people – but she was still sticking around, at least for now. In fact she had promptly been hired as the public face of a local construction company. "They need black females," she sometimes joked of the corporate world. But the laughter only half-masked her frustration. She didn't rule out returning to the law one day.

Then early in the new year, after a big family Christmas, Marie van der Westhuizen had cycled over to her grandfather's house to take him breakfast. Finding the gates locked and hearing no reply to her shouts, she'd climbed over the fence and gone upstairs. There she found the rich, grouchy owner of Bulrush farm, but a man who'd always been kind to her, more like a father really since Boeta had always been so busy on the farm, lying peacefully in his bed, dead at the age of seventy-five. Probably from an aneurism.

It was almost exactly two years since Oom Loedie had found Simon and Samuel waiting at his gate. Now he would never know what price his only son and grandson would pay for what had happened next.

Ten days later razor-minded, dry-humoured Nico Dreyer, who had been wheelchair-bound for many months, died in Bloemfontein at the age of fifty-four. He'd been a fine rugby player once. Most of the accused and their families travelled to the city from Parys for the funeral of the man who, many felt, had offered them the best chance of navigating a safe route through this tortuous trial. Now they'd have to find someone new to replace him; and not Kobus Burger – a good man, they all insisted, but damaged in court by the malicious claim that he'd told the farmers to destroy evidence.

In February, Simon Jubeba's grandmother died. Norma Jubeba had spent the last few years of her life lying in the back room of the family home in Tumahole, just across the road from the dump, weakened by a stroke and unable to talk. They'd buried her on a Saturday. A good crowd. Because everyone knew each other, it somehow felt like Tumahole was always having funerals. More than in Parys.

It was a whole year since the trial proper had started. Now it was time for proceedings to resume. As the courtroom began to fill up, the news flitted along the chilly benches. "They tell us the fat lawyer died," Ruth said with a shrug. There had been another death too: Jerry, the court translator, had just buried his son in Soweto. His wife had died the year before. And now someone had poisoned Ruth's dog, Romeo. She wouldn't be able to leave anything outside the shack at night in case thieves came. They'd already stolen her pumpkins.

*

The courtroom was transfixed by the sounds of frantic electronic clicks and a low, murmuring buzz. Captain Henk Prinsloo's portable shocking device had taken centre stage. His lawyer had brought in the police captain's privately owned device – a sleek, black, hand-held metal tube with a torch at one end surrounded by a serrated metal ring. After some inept fiddling by the lawyer, Prinsloo was allowed to show the court how, by pressing a button on the side, the instrument emitted its staccato shocks from the same end as the torch. There were nervous giggles as it was passed up to the judge and then to the prosecution.

Prinsloo had bought the device with his own money some years earlier. He kept it in a pocket in the front of his bullet-proof jacket. It was a handy thing to have – especially at road-blocks – but you needed to keep it fully charged and that night, when he'd gone out to investigate the farm attack, he'd only just returned from a long sick-leave after injuring his arm. The torch still just about worked, but the shocker was flat – completely dead.

So yes, he'd taken the device with him when he'd gone over to look at the two black men lying in the back of Anton's pickup, but only as a torch. He'd splashed water in the men's faces, had even given one of them a drink. They both had swollen faces but Prinsloo hadn't seen any real bleeding or open wounds. In fact he'd had a conversation with one of them – the one lying on his back, the one who'd asked for a drink.

What's your name? Prinsloo had asked.

Simon mumbled something.

Where's the gun?

Water. Simon wanted to drink.

Where's the gun?

Simon pointed towards Samuel, slumped near him.

He had the gun. He threw it away.

Prinsloo remembered all this. The blood in the pickup. Dried blood on Simon's lips. A small scratch near his mouth. But giving him an electric shock? Nonsense. There was nothing to gain from that. Maybe a jab in the ribs. Nothing more.

In court, the prosecution now called its last witnesses – Isaac Xhalisa and Thomas Direko, the black workers sent to the scene by Kobus Dannhauser, the portly chairman of the local farmers' union, who had been away on holiday at the time. Both men described watching Prinsloo reach over the side of Anton's pickup, take a shocking device from his belt, and push it into Simon's private parts.

"He was asking him questions while shocking him," Direko said, mimicking the action.

But Direko and Xhalisa both insisted that the shocker they'd seen was not the one Prinsloo produced in court – that in fact the policeman had held a torch in one hand and a cattle-prod in the other. They even sketched the cattle-prod for the court – a fatter, stubbier device with two metal rods protruding from one end. The prosecution brought one of these into court and demonstrated how it was activated by being pushed into a solid object, triggering a low, steady electronic buzzing noise.

"I know this shocker because I'm working with it, with the cattle that I'm handling," Xhalisa said. "The torch is different. The shocker has two points at the front."

At this moment it was the judge who intervened. During his evidence, Ockert van Zyl had testified that he had not heard Captain Prinsloo's shocking device making any sound when it was applied to the man in the pickup. Now the judge wanted to know if these new witnesses had heard anything.

"Did you see or hear any shocking sounds?" she asked.

"No, My Lady," Xhalisa replied.

"So what makes you say 'shock'?"

"I say that because the accused took it out and put it on the private parts."

In the dock, Prinsloo slowly shook his head.

"Over his underpants?"

"Yes."

"But was the shocker even working?"

"I do not know."

In their separate testimonies, Xhalisa and Direko would both insist that the fact that Simon had not twitched, or shouted out, or made any reaction when he was being prodded by the device was proof that he must have been unconscious.

"I'm saying you could tell, because the body didn't move," Xhalisa said.

Again the judge wondered whether it might equally be proof that the device wasn't working.

"I don't know if it was working or not," Direko conceded, his head lowered as though he'd become allergic to eye contact.

Why Direko seemed so determined to assume the worst of Captain Prinsloo was puzzling. Was it because he and Xhalisa had recognised the two men in the back of Anton's bakkie — had known Simon and Samuel for years — and felt angry about the beatings the men had received and angry with all those white men standing around in the darkness showing no hint of concern or regret? Or was it more complicated than that?

Prinsloo remembered what Direko had said to him and the farmers that night, and it wasn't "Stop!" or "Leave these men alone, they've had enough." Instead, standing in the group beside the vehicle, looking at Simon lying flat on his back and struggling for breath, Direko — trusted foreman on the biggest farm in the district — had turned to the whites with a practical suggestion.

"Give that man to me and you'll never see him again."

That was what Captain Prinsloo remembered. It rang true with Kobus Burger too — from his perspective blacks in Direko's position on the farms were often as violent, or more violent, than their white bosses.

And there was something else, something that made Direko's evidence against the police captain even more questionable.

A few months before the killings, Fanie Oosthuizen had stumbled on an awkward scene. The old railway line that ran east from Parys, out past the Weiveld crossroads and deep into the farms, had been derelict for years, but the rusting rails themselves were still extremely valuable to anyone with the inclination and the equipment necessary to pull them up – and the right buyer. It was theft, of course. A long prison sentence for anyone caught. But everyone in the district claimed to know that Tom Direko had been stockpiling and selling the rails for a year or more, and one afternoon during the harvest, as Fanie was inspecting a field that the Van der Westhuizens were leasing from Dannhauser at the time, he spotted a big pile of rails at the back, under some trees.

"You're a crook," Fanie had told Direko. He was joking really – it was none of his business what Tom got up to. Although it was a bad example to set the workers on all the other farms. Direko agreed but he told Fanie it wasn't his idea. He was doing it for the boss. And then a truck turned up, one of those ones they use to transport vegetables, and the white driver started loading the rails onto the truck. Fanie, always the joker, started taking photos on his phone, just messing around, to wind Tom up a little more. But the driver got nervous and called the Dannhausers.

Fanie was in trouble. He was in even more trouble four hours later when the police arrived – the Hawks – a big team of them. The truck had already left, but they arrested Thomas Direko and several others. Even though Fanie swore it wasn't him who'd blown the whistle, that he'd just been larking around with the photo-taking, they still blamed him.

But the real twist had come a few months later, soon after the killings of Simon and Samuel, when Captain Laux and the Hawks came looking for Direko, to take his statement and do the ID parade.

The day after Thomas Direko picked Captain Prinsloo out of that line-up, the charges that were still pending against him for the rail theft were – the policeman claimed – dropped.

"All of a sudden, after I was pointed out at the ID parade, that case was withdrawn," Prinsloo observed drily. "You can think what you want to think."

*

J.J. Mlotshwa was nearly done. On balance, he thought the prosecution had made a good case, maybe not strong enough to win six murder convictions, but that was always going to be a struggle. Some of the youngsters might get away with aggravated assault and that was fine by Mlotshwa.

The farmworker, Xhalisa, was still on the stand. A slim man in a black tracksuit top with a shaved head.

"You could see he was breathing heavily, slowly," Xhalisa said, describing Simon lying in the bakkie. "The one who was leaning against the cab, Tjixa, was breathing heavily from the mouth. I turned and left the bakkie."

"I hear you're saying a name," Mlotshwa said, sounding almost startled.

After weeks in court, this was the first time Samuel's surname had been mentioned and it seemed to catch the prosecution by surprise.

"Shika? Tjenka?" Mlotshwa inquired politely. "Can you spell it or write it down?"

Ruth had come to court that day and so had her son Lawrence. Silent, contemplative, unemployed, uncomplaining, gentle

Lawrence, still trying to sort out his C.V., still stuck at home, while Elias had already found new work at the abattoir.

Suddenly there was a noise from the back row. Someone was on his feet, not exactly shouting, but something close, something that was, for him, the equivalent of a scream of protest.

"Tjixa!" Lawrence said, and then again, more quietly this time, already starting to sit down. "Tjixa."

25

A SLAP AND A KICK

AT HOME, BOETA was drinking harder than ever. Sometimes he took his medication – for anxiety and depression – and sometimes he didn't. Or he gulped down far too many pills and wandered around the house for hours, confused about the simplest things. The trial had hit another snag, and he was taking his frustration out on his family. It was becoming unbearable for everyone.

One evening, he was grumbling at Rikki, complaining that he felt abandoned by his own relatives, and then things suddenly escalated. Marie could hear the racket from her bedroom. Boeta started arguing with his son about the farm and, when Rikki tried to intervene, her husband began screaming, swearing, saying crazy stuff, telling his wife to get the fuck out of his house. "I've ruined your lives!" he shouted. "There's nothing to keep you here – no reason for you to stay with me. So pack your stuff and go. No-one is here for me. You're nothing to me now!"

Then he dragged his wife to the door and pushed her out into the mid-winter night. He told the kids to leave too. Then he slammed the door shut and locked it.

It was not the first time – and Rikki now had to admit it to herself – her husband had been violent. Standing in the yard outside beside one of the tractors, she realised a decision had been made for her.

"He told me to go, and I did," she reflected later, stirring a cup of tea on the porch of the Plum Tree Café in town. Loedie had taken his mother and sister over to Crista's house and then driven off into the night. The next morning Rikki came to collect some clothes, and then she and Marie drove into town to stay with a friend. Within days, Marie was back in hospital being treated for depression.

Soon Boeta was phoning, pleading with Rikki to come home. But the answer was no.

"There is only so much you can do," Rikki said.

*

The courtroom snag that delayed the trial and helped push Boeta over the edge was, in a sense, his own fault.

On the thirty-seventh day of the trial he'd finally been called by the defence to testify.

Accused number 1. Solemn, unreadable.

A rainstorm was battering the courthouse roof as he'd lumbered towards the witness box.

"I'm forty-eight. I'm a farmer. Loedie is my son. He's accused number 5." Then, in a monotone, Boeta had proceeded to map out his version of events – his fury that evening in the field, how he'd lost his head, had charged straight over to a man he immediately recognised as Simon, a former employee he'd sacked for stealing sausages. How he'd been thinking about his bloodied father, and about Mrs Van Rooyen stuffed in that freezer. How he'd kicked Simon hard in the chest then crouched over him, screaming about the missing gun, throwing punches at the man's face. How he'd called for someone to bring him a pistol, which he'd then pointed at Simon's face and cocked. And then how he tried to hit him with it, but Simon had kept blocking with his arm and the gun had broken into pieces.

Boeta spoke steadily, blandly, like a man who'd rehearsed the words so often he hardly recognised their meaning. He denied later threatening to cut out the youngsters' tongues if they co-operated with the police. He was finished before lunch, and the court adjourned.

After the lunch break the prosecution began its cross-examination.

Throughout the course of the trial, the six accused had used the same lawyer, partly to save money, but also because the men insisted that their stories were all aligned, that they were allies in this fight, each reinforcing the others' version of events. But when J.J. Mlotshwa began probing Boeta's memory of what had happened to the two men in the back of Anton's pickup that night, something shifted. Perhaps accidentally, or perhaps Boeta knew exactly what he was doing. Perhaps he was trying, subtly, to shift blame from himself and onto his oldest friend.

"After I tapped him, he spoke," Boeta said. He was describing the moment he'd hit Simon with a fan-belt in the bakkie, the action that another witness, Ockert Van Zyl, had described as being vicious – 'like dogs on a hare'. In Boeta's version, he had merely tapped the man on the face, then had some sort of conversation with him. And then he had left the scene to take the dogs home to Oom Loedie's place.

"So you saw no injuries on him?" the prosecutor jumped in.

"No."

Mlotshwa showed the court a photograph of Simon, slumped on his side in the bakkie, with his trousers pulled down to his knees, exposing a pair of green underpants. At which point Boeta observed that Simon had not been in that position when he'd left the field, that his trousers had not been pulled down, that the photo had been taken some twenty minutes after he'd departed, that something had changed. Perhaps something important.

"But accused numbers 2 and 3 were still there when you left?" asked the prosecutor.

"Yes."

"And 4?"

"Yes."

"So they can explain what happened to that man ..." Mlotshwa suggested.

"I can't speak for them," Boeta said.

That was it. Enough – more than enough – reason for the state prosecutor to ask the judge to halt the trial. Two days later, the defence team reluctantly conceded that a "possible conflict of interest" had emerged between Boeta van der Westhuizen and Anton Loggenberg. For the trial to proceed, all the defence lawyers would have to withdraw from the case and an entirely new, expanded team would need to be hired to represent the accused, this time as individuals.

Anton's wife, Gusta, stood up briskly and walked out of

court. Was Boeta about to betray them too, like all the other farmers?

"Well, we'll see," she muttered.

In the courtyard outside, Cor and Miela stood, dazed, and in tears. Once again, their lives were to be put on hold. Captain Prinsloo put a hand on Cor's shoulder. The policeman was wondering how he could possibly afford his own lawyer now – legal aid was his only option.

Kobus Burger paced between the accused, trying to offer comfort, but he was seething with a more generalised sense of injustice that stretched far beyond South Africa. Building up a head of steam, he began describing how Muslims were deliberately provoking conflicts in the Middle East in order to give them an excuse to flee to the West.

"They'll take over Europe within a decade," he said, climbing into his car. "Mark my words. And don't think I've disappeared off the edge of the earth. They didn't get rid of me."

*

And so the trial was put on pause once again. In town, Rikki kept busy at work. She'd had her job at the epilepsy charity in Parys for six years now, helping to care for fifty or so adults, referred from all over the Free State, with a range of psychiatric and mental conditions, and living in a collection of small, tidy buildings one block back from the river. The pay was low, but the work was steady and rewarding and the management had continued to allow her to take unpaid leave to attend court.

After a fortnight, Marie had been discharged from the hospital, but she found it hard to go back to school. One friend, a cousin, had remained loyal, but the taunts kept coming from the other white kids. Murderer's child. By and large, she found the black kids were far less cruel. Maybe they didn't know the whole story. Or, more likely, they just chose to keep quiet. Marie was nearly sixteen now and had made two big decisions. She wanted to study law. And she wanted to get the hell out of Parys, away from her family, away from the whole Van der Westhuizen clan, and all the rest of it, as soon as possible.

*

It was almost nine months before a new defence team was assembled, briefed, and ready to resume the trial. On a mild morning in late January 2019, Boeta straightened his back in the witness box, turned his head towards his co-accused in the dock with the juddering intensity of a man wrestling with his own nervous system, and then glanced behind them, towards the public benches. He seemed like a different man. His cheek muscles were twitching and tears were snaking down towards his jaw. He brushed his left eye roughly with the back of his hand, then swallowed hard, twice.

"My marriage has broken down," he said quietly. A few yards away from him, Rikki almost held his eye, then took out a tissue to blow her nose. "These past three years have broken my life. We are all broken. We have cried our hearts out. All of us." He found it too painful to talk about Marie's struggles, but he looked over at his son, Loedie, who had slumped below the level of the dock, his head almost between his knees. "My son has been trying to build a wall around himself. We've had difficulty talking. It's been hard for me as a father, knowing that I couldn't help him through this time."

Boeta looked at the judge, then the lawyer, then back towards the public gallery where Ruth sat. "I want to tell the families of the deceased that I am very sorry. I'm sorry about what happened on that day, and sorry for the part I played in it."

He spoke of his shock at hearing the 204s' damning testimony.

"These were my blood relatives. It was stunning what they said against us."

For a moment, it felt like Boeta had come back to life. The monotone was gone. His face an open look. But it didn't last long. Under cross-examination, he became guarded once again and almost sullen.

"I don't know," he kept saying. "I didn't see."

Even the judge appeared to raise an eyebrow when Boeta repeatedly insisted that he had not seen his son Loedie at the scene.

"Not at all?" the judge asked.

"No."

"Did he tell you later what he did at the scene?"

"Not in any detail."

"I'm having difficulty understanding ..." the judge tailed off as a cloud of scepticism seemed to envelop the courtroom. Here was a father protecting his son. The crime scene had been crowded with farmers, but somehow Boeta had noticed almost no-one.

When the prosecutor returned to the scene in the back of Anton's white pickup – where Simon and Samuel lay, badly bruised and breathing heavily – Boeta said he assumed they were still out of breath from having run across the fields. Another prosecutor might have challenged such an account, but J.J. Mlotshwa let it pass, along with many other unanswered questions. Boeta was not even asked about the actions of his best friend, Anton.

Then, abruptly, the cross-examination was over.

Rikki moved towards the dock and Boeta – his face, his posture, his whole presence now visibly relaxing – put his arm round her and stroked her back. It was a small, brief gesture, but it hinted at an evolving compromise in the Van der Westhuizens' home. Now that the trial had resumed, Rikki had decided to move back to the farmhouse with Marie, so she could keep an eye on everyone. It was the role she'd always played. For now, Boeta needed "babysitting", she said. The rest could wait. Family came first. "I'm not giving up. When we're being attacked from the outside, then we must all come together," she explained, before turning back to the public bench to collect an empty picnic bag.

*

Two days later, Henk Prinsloo sat in a chair at a guesthouse in Parys, rolled up his shirt sleeve, paused for a moment, and then pushed a grey cattle-prod sharply into his left forearm. The two steel rods clicked back into the handle and immediately released almost 250 000 thousand volts into the police captain's slim frame. Prinsloo felt the pain like a fizzing slap to his body. His neck muscles locked and he was overcome by a shudder of nausea.

The men around him – the new team of defence lawyers who'd gathered to observe the experiment together with a retired forensic expert – all chuckled.

We must call you Sparky! the expert said.

In court the following week Henk Prinsloo showed the judge his injuries. The painful experiment had evidently been designed to help prove to the court that Prinsloo could not have shocked Simon or Samuel that night, that such a violent act would have left clear signs on their flesh, unmistakably visible at their post-mortems. And perhaps there was a subtler intention too – that of an accused man so anxious to persuade a judge that he was wronged and innocent that he wanted her to know he was prepared to torture himself to clear his name.

But over the weekend, the two small circular blisters had begun to fade. By the time Prinsloo rolled his sleeve up in court, they were too faint to be identifiable. Besides – as the judge remarked – on darker skin, they would have been even harder to spot.

And so Prinsloo pushed on with his testimony.

"I received a telephone call at 18:24," he said in his quiet voice. "I put myself on duty, put on my uniform ... fetched my bullet-proof jacket and vehicle ..." He explained how he'd been the first policeman to arrive at the scene, had immediately met Boeta and Anton, and had gone over to see the suspects, who were lying in the back of Anton Loggenberg's pickup.

"I asked him his name. He answered but I couldn't hear him clearly. I went to the other man and poured some water on him too. He looked at me and made a sound – like 'hegh-hegh'." Prinsloo pretended to cough. To the policeman, the two black suspects did not appear seriously injured. Bruised, yes. A small scratch or two, perhaps, and some swelling. But nothing that required urgent medical attention. One of them – it was Simon – had even managed to say a few words to Prinsloo, and later, when both men had fallen quiet, the policeman still saw no reason for concern.

"It looked to me as if they were sleeping," he said.

*

Prinsloo's new advocate, a legal aid lawyer named Dawie Reynecke, asked him if he'd used the shocker on either suspect.

"No! It would be shameful," Prinsloo replied. He had poked both men in the ribs to get their attention. Nothing more. Then how to explain Boeta's joking threat to "hit" Prinsloo if he touched him with that same shocking device – a dual purpose torch and electric prodder? The policeman agreed with Boeta's explanation now. They had been referring to the instrument's torch, not its shocking function. After all, he said, "a torch can burn you if it's hot."

J.J. Mlotshwa allowed himself a small, sceptical sigh, pushed his glasses back up the bridge of his nose with his left hand, and stared hard at the policeman.

"So, all these people are lying about what you did?" the prosecutor asked, when his turn came to cross-examine.

"Yes," Prinsloo replied, his back straight, indignation prickling on his face. A prodder always makes a loud tell-tale buzz. No-one had heard a buzz. And no-one had seen Simon or Samuel move – even an unconscious person would have moved when jolted by so many volts.

These were compelling arguments. Big obstacles for the prosecution to overcome.

Why, Mlotshwa asked the police captain, would three state witnesses – Ockert van Zyl, Thomas Direko, Isaac Xhalisa – lie?

Prinsloo was ready with his answer. He dismissed Van Zyl, with contempt, as a mere fantasist. Then he spelled out his theory about Thomas Direko and his colleague Isaac Xhalisa. They had told the Hawks what they wanted to hear, he maintained, in exchange for having the prior theft charges against Direko dropped.

A corrupt stitch-up was a serious allegation but Mlotshwa had a letter from the prosecution service, which he then produced, that seemed to confirm that those theft charges against Direko had in fact been dropped weeks *before* the killings. In other words, Prinsloo's conspiracy theory had to be wrong.

"So, you did nothing wrong at the scene that night?" the prosecutor now asked in a gentler tone.

"Correct."

"No reason to be remorseful? For anything?"

"No."

Mlotshwa nodded thoughtfully. Then he wondered aloud why the next two policemen to arrive at the field, perhaps an hour after Prinsloo, had immediately recognised the seriousness of the two men's injuries and had called for an ambulance right away. In fact, one of the men, a black officer named Jerry Matloane, had told the Hawks that he was so shocked by their condition, and so angered by the "joking" of the white farmers, that he'd left the scene and refused to help move Simon and Samuel into the police van. It was Mlotshwa's last line of attack.

Prinsloo's response was an almost physical one. He hesitated. For a moment he even seemed to shrink in the witness box. When he began to speak it was to play down his role that evening, on January 6, 2016. He was merely a "first responder", he explained, at an "arrest scene", who had no medical training, was not a detective, or an investigator. He could hardly have been expected to juggle so many duties and simultaneously assess the physical condition of two alleged criminals. His task had been to "secure" the scene and to wait for more senior, more experienced colleagues to arrive.

The prosecutor pointed out that the next two officers to join him were both more junior in rank than Captain Prinsloo.

"Yes, that's true," Prinsloo conceded.

And that was it.

J.J. Mlotshwa sat down in his chair and turned to his colleague with a small smile of satisfaction. The murder charge against Prinsloo seemed, at best, shaky. But another point had been well made: that a highly experienced police officer had entirely mistaken his duty that night. He had arrived at what he assumed to be an arrest scene and, perhaps blinded by his good relations with the white farmers, had fallen in with their assessment of the situation without questioning it. Here were two wretched thieves who'd taken a little beating. His priority as a police officer was to help trace the criminals' footprints back to Loedie van der Westhuizen's farm.

In doing so Prinsloo had failed to see what was immediately obvious to his less experienced colleagues: that this was, self-evidently, far more than a mere arrest scene.

While Prinsloo had been bustling around with the farmers, two men had been quietly dying. Right in front of him.

*

Two blocks from the courthouse, on the porch of A.B.'s bar, half a dozen Afrikaner men in white shirts and dark ties tucked energetically into their steaks.

They were the new defence team.

The lawyer for Miela Janse van Rensburg, accused number 6, was a short, cheerful man called Hennie du Plessis. He was already starting to turn his attention back to another case he'd been involved in – the "sunflower murders", as the media had dubbed them, in nearby Coligny. The recent sentencing in that case had alarmed the accused in Parys and their families. The two white farm workers had been found guilty of murdering the sixteen-year-old boy and had been sentenced to eighteen and twenty-three years in prison respectively.

It seemed ominous.

"Political," Rikki muttered, of the judgment.

The Coligny men had been convicted on the strength of one eyewitness. But Hennie du Plessis, who had been defending one of the white men, had argued in court that the eyewitness was lying. And now, he said, he had discovered that the witness had confessed to two local pastors that he had indeed made up his story about seeing the white men throw the boy off their bakkie. There were suggestions that the witness had been bribed. For the white farming community, it really did feel like a political stitch-up. The men's lawyers were preparing an appeal.

*

In Parys, by contrast, the defence team were feeling much more confident about the case they'd unexpectedly inherited. So confident that they were now advising the four clients who had not yet testified – Loedie, Miela, Cor and Anton – to adopt a bold new strategy: plead guilty to assault and decline to testify in court. After all, the state had failed to make its case, so why give the prosecution a chance to cross-examine them?

Anton held out for a night – "I need to sleep on it, to dream on it," he grumbled – but in the morning he agreed.

He stood in the dock in court and listened as his lawyer read out the briefest of confessions.

"I approached one of the suspects. I kicked him in the hip area to draw his attention ... I slapped the one suspect (not the one that I kicked) to draw his attention, on the shoulder. It was never my intention to kill any of the suspects nor to seriously injure any of them."

That was it. A slap and a kick.

Next came Cor. He stood while his lawyer read out a similar statement.

"I struck the man on his shin with the cane with the intent to injure him. After striking him once, I moved away."

Then it was the turn of Klein Loedie's lawyer.

"I assaulted two unknown male persons ... by hitting the first with an open hand, kicking the second at his hip and instilling fear to the first by striking blows with my monkey-wrench next to his head. I, however, did not assault either with the intent to cause them any grievous bodily harm."

Last to confess was Miela. His lawyer read out his statement. Simon and Samuel had both said the other was to blame for attacking the old man. As he was standing over "the first suspect" and "tapping" him on the shoulder with his torch, the man had gestured towards his friend and said "'He said we should kill the old man.' I assaulted an unknown male person ... by kicking him twice with a booted foot ... directed towards the area of his right hip."

The statements having been read out and admissions made, the accused sat and waited.

26

STONE DEAD

W HAT HAD PROMPTED this new strategy on the part of
the defence team?

It all came down to the medical evidence.

It started with the question of the two black men being
transported, unsecured, in the back of the police van.

It continued when they arrived by ambulance at Parys
Hospital.

The defence team had come to the conclusion that the state
had failed "dismally" to link the alleged actions of the accused
to any specific wounds on Simon and Samuel's bodies. The
prosecution's case was "a circus", the lawyers said. Mlotshwa's
logic was "naïve", and "simplistic". And to hammer that point
home, they called one final witness to testify.

Professor Jan Botha was the man who'd given Prinsloo
the nickname "Sparky". He had recently retired after an
illustrious career in forensic medicine. A burly man with a
creased face, he'd conducted more than forty thousand autopsies and, as his eight-page curriculum vitae attested, had been
one of the country's most experienced and senior pathologists.
Now he sat in the witness box and gamely tore into the state's
case and, specifically, into the two autopsies conducted by

Dr Lairi – the man who'd compared the case to Steve Biko's murder.

"These are two high-profile autopsies done in an academic unit. The standard is ... to my mind, totally inadequate," Botha said. He then proceeded to go through Lairi's work like a gruff teacher marking a particularly feeble exam paper. Lairi had failed to make basic notes, had skipped procedures, had failed to weigh the men's internal organs, had failed to shave their heads, had drawn flawed and "somewhat bizarre" conclusions, had missed at least one significant laceration altogether, and had, overall, given the impression of merely "glancing" at the bodies. He had done less than the "bare minimum" expected of a properly trained pathologist – which, Botha reminded the court, Dr Lairi was not.

"It raises questions about the thoroughness of the examination and therefore the credibility of the entire autopsy," he concluded, witheringly, before moving to address the specific allegations against the accused, starting with the claim that Boeta had smashed the pistol into Simon's head.

"I would have expected an imprint type of abrasion, reflecting the weapon used. I can't see any injury ... that correlates with that."

The same held true for Anton, and the allegation that he'd trampled on Samuel's skull with all his 195-kilogram bulk.

"It would have been a good balancing act if he could do it!"

The defence team couldn't help chuckling at that image, but Jerry, the court interpreter, glancing towards Ruth and Selina on the public benches, chose to leave the comment untranslated.

"If the full weight of the accused had been brought to bear on his head there would probably be a concomitant skull fracture," Botha said, once the laughter had died down.

Boeta's son, Loedie, had been accused of hitting the side of Samuel's – or possibly Simon's – head with a large monkey-wrench, but again, the professor insisted that such an action would have left obvious injuries. "My Lady, this is a heavy object ... if force was applied vigorously I would expect the face to be totally crushed."

As for the heavy blows that Cor was accused of landing with a large walking stick, the kierie – there was no evidence of that whatsoever.

"If such a blow was administered, it was a very light blow."

Botha was equally unpersuaded by evidence concerning the men's broken ribs – injuries that the state wanted to link to the kicks that Boeta, Loedie and Miela all admitted they'd given. Dr Lairi had, in his conclusions, suggested those injuries could have played a part in the deaths.

"Nonsense," was the professor's professional opinion. Both men died solely from their head injuries, injuries that could well have been caused by the bumpy journey in the back of the police van.

"Sliding or rolling around in the back of the vehicle ... unable to steady or protect themselves ... I believe, for example, a hard blow or contact with one of the seat supports could either cause a fatal head injury or significantly aggravate a pre-existing injury."

The professor was not asked about the 204s. But his evidence seemed to imply that it was at least as likely that Muller and his cousins and colleagues had delivered the fatal blows to Simon and Samuel. In other words, the wrong people might well be on trial.

In the sunshine outside court, one of the defence lawyers voiced his conviction that Jan Botha's testimony had been decisive.

"The state's case is stone dead," he declared.

*

It had been Sister Margaret Mafubelu's fourth nightshift in a row.

Giving evidence when she'd been called to the witness stand at the trial of the white farmers, she'd struggled to recall every detail, but she remembered standing outside in the dark on the night of January 6, 2016, watching an ambulance drive up to Casualty. She remembered the paramedics wheeling those two poor men into the brightly lit hallway.

Unknown Male One.

Unknown Male Two.

She'd been the one to label them like that, since the police officers accompanying them had no other information. She could see the paramedics had been busy on the drive back from where the men had been transferred from the police van because both casualties had neck braces, oxygen masks, and bandages obscuring their swollen heads.

Casualty had been enjoying a relatively quiet evening after a fortnight of drunken fights and accidents and other associated side-effects of the festive season. Just one asthma case, a couple of dehydrations, a headache and two abdominal pains.

The ambulance driver had called ahead to alert the Casualty staff. Sister Margaret and her colleagues knew it was something to do with a farm attack, but still she wondered when she saw the condition they were in: what must these two have done to deserve such a beating?

Unknown Male One was "very, very restless". She had to lift up the bars on the side of the bed to stop him falling out. He was twitching and shaking, and breathing in fast, low gasps. Head injury, she thought to herself. She already knew, or suspected, that he wasn't going to make it. Sister Margaret pinched him hard on the arm – no reaction. She spoke to him, asking his name – again no response. She shone a torch into his eyes – one pupil dilated, neither eye reacting to the light. Using the internal phone network she immediately called the only doctor on duty at the hospital that night.

Dr Sifiso Nxumalo was a stern, ponderous man. At 10.15 p.m. he walked over to Casualty from the maternity ward. He noted the presence of a policeman and a detective standing near the two stretchers. Then he listened to the nurse's assessment.

The Glasgow Coma Scale has been used internationally for decades to assess the neurological condition of patients. An alert, fully conscious person should score fifteen points. Anything less than eight means the person is unlikely to be able to breathe without assistance and needs intubating and rushing to the nearest emergency medical centre. Dr Nxumalo briefly repeated Sister Margaret's tests but he had already concluded she was correct – those black eyes – the raccoon-eyes – were a giveaway.

Unknown Male One had a G.C.S. score of three.

The doctor stitched up the gash on the man's head and told the nurses to give him antibiotics and to prepare to intubate him. Soon afterwards he made a call to a trauma unit in Bloemfontein and then to the control room of a private ambulance service in Kroonstad.

Is that necessary? one of the policemen asked. Both of the patients were under arrest. They needed to be questioned.

*

At 7.00 a.m. the following morning, Unknown Male One – heavily sedated, with a breathing tube down his throat – was pushed through the doors of the Pelonomi Hospital in Bloemfontein. Almost nine hours had passed since he'd first been assessed in Parys and the gravity and urgency of his condition recognised.

A slim man with short black hair and glasses, and an earnest expression, Dr Werner van Tonder was coming to the end of a quiet overnight shift. There were only three other patients in the trauma department – one of them with a fractured skull from a machete attack – and all had been stabilised. Van Tonder had been expecting the case from Parys for several hours already. He couldn't understand why it had taken so long for the ambulance to get there, especially with a patient with a suspected brain injury. The first hour or two were always crucial.

The truth was that, somehow, it had taken the nurses and ambulance crew in Parys nearly three hours to intubate the patient and transfer him over to the ambulance's intubation system. Had the driver then set off and either turned north on the motorway towards Soweto, Johannesburg, or cut across the crater's edge further west, towards Potchefstroom, he could have reached a major hospital in either of those places in under an hour. Instead, governed by strict rules requiring medical treatment to remain within individual provinces, the driver turned south, towards the Free State's capital, Bloemfontein, which was some 300 kilometres away.

In court, almost two years later, he explained that there were trucks clogging the motorway and so he had taken the back roads. It took six hours to reach his destination.

The body on Dr van Tonder's table made him think of a car crash victim. So many signs of violence. He could feel a big crack in the man's skull, from just above his eye and round towards his ear. It was a wonder the team in Parys had thought it worthwhile sending him all this way when the patient was clearly brain dead and, in the dry terminology of the medical profession, "unsalvageable". That's what three out of fifteen on the G.C.S. meant. There was nothing more to be done. They took an X-ray and a C.T. scan and did a blood test for form's sake, checked the man's catheter and wrapped him in a thermal blanket. After some time, they took him off the ventilator.

At 11.05 a.m. on the morning of January 7, 2016, stripped of the intubation equipment, his bruised head still impossibly round, a neatly cropped moustache visible above his swollen lips, Unknown Male One – as yet unidentified as Simon Jubeba – was declared dead.

*

In Parys Hospital, Samuel Tjixa, naked except for a pair of bright red underpants, was trying to speak.

"Eh. Ehh."

"What's your name?" Sister Margaret asked him.

"Uh." His eyelids fluttered and he tried to look round the room, but his swollen mouth could not form words. She could see he was in better shape than the other man, but not that much better. If this one survives, she thought to herself, he'll be a cabbage.

Dr Nxumalo hadn't got around to seeing Samuel until almost midnight. He noted the heavy bruising and the abrasions on the patient's chest, and the swelling on his face and head, but seemed eager to give him the most optimistic possible assessment. He prescribed headache tablets and something to reduce inflammation, and decided, given the late hour, that it was worth admitting the patient so that he could have some X-rays in the morning to check on what seemed like a minor head injury. Dr Nxumalo told a nurse to give the man some pethidine – a heavy sedative – and Samuel quickly fell into a deep sleep. The doctor recorded in his notes that the patient's Glasgow Coma Scale was probably fourteen out of fifteen, or maybe even a perfect fifteen.

Samuel was wheeled into the general ward at 1.30 a.m., accompanied by two student nurses and a police officer, who was keen to put handcuffs on the suspect but was eventually persuaded that, having been sedated, Unknown Male Two was unlikely to escape from the hospital. They could talk to him in the morning.

At 4.00 a.m., Nurse Mantoa Lefatle came over to check on

Samuel for the first time in two and a half hours and noted some significant changes. The patient was now struggling for air, his eyes were swollen firmly closed and blood was trickling from his nose. Nurse Lefatle later insisted that she'd immediately called Dr Nxumalo and told him he was needed, urgently.

The doctor, however, was busy "with some other emergencies" in the Casualty ward. It was "hectic" there. He promised to come as soon as possible.

An hour later the nurse checked on Samuel again. This time he was gasping, heavily and slowly. His blood pressure had fallen dramatically and a brownish discharge was pouring from his mouth and nose. Another call was made to Dr Nxumalo. He really should come immediately.

At 6.00 a.m. as Dr Nxumalo later described it, he "rushed" into the general ward to examine Samuel, who was lying on a metal hospital bed on a child-size white bedsheet that was covered with drawings of a bear playing with two balloons and didn't quite reach the end of a pink water-proof mattress.

The doctor and nurse had different recollections of those next few moments on the ward. Nurse Lefatle said Samuel was still alive when Dr Nxumalo stood over him and that the patient was still "gasping".

Dr Nxumalo said he'd come too late. In court he'd stated that there was "no spontaneous breathing, no palpable pulse, no heart rate. Then I certified the patient deceased."

In fact, Dr Nxumalo had not struck many people in court as a compelling or credible witness. He seemed to misunderstand the simplest questions and was repeatedly asked by the judge to listen more carefully and to answer with greater clarity. The defence lawyers had privately mocked his halting, ponderous, sometimes indecipherable testimony, arguing between themselves about how to rate the doctor's own Glasgow Coma Scale while in the witness box. Kobus Burger had chuckled and said he deserved three out of fifteen. A colleague reckoned it was minus two.

Under cross-examination Dr Nxumalo struggled to explain how he could have given Unknown Male Two a G.C.S. of fourteen when, as his own notes showed, the patient was "not able to communicate".

"I would say ... er ... with due respect ... I made ... er ... a mistake in terms of that," he conceded.

He also acknowledged that, had he responded to the nurse's calls earlier in the night, things might have turned out differently.

"I made mistakes."

The suspicion, privately articulated by the defence team but never raised in open court, was that the doctor, rather than being tied up with other emergencies on a "hectic" Casualty ward, had been fast asleep, and that the nursing staff had lied to cover up for his negligence.

When later asked directly by a journalist if the doctor had, indeed, been sleeping, Sister Margaret exhaled, made a face that seemed to say Well, obviously, but then said, "I can't comment on that. I'm sorry."

27

ALMOST INEXPLICABLE

IT WAS THE last day of the trial and Ruth, who had grown weary of attending every day, had been summoned, unexpectedly, to appear as a witness. Her mobile had recently been stolen and the police had forgotten where she lived, so a reporter took her to Parys. She sat silently in the car for the half-hour journey, scratching furiously at some mosquito bites on her legs and wondering what these people wanted with her now, all this time later, and whether what she now referred to as her "old wounds" were going to be reopened. It was too much.

An hour later she was sitting in the witness stand, brusquely dabbing her eyes with a yellow handkerchief, as a series of police photographs were put in front of her.

The judge had requested Ruth's presence – along with that of Simon Jubeba's aunts, Paulina and Selina – to try to clear up a confusion that had obstinately endured in court through the trial.

Which deceased was Samuel Tjixa, and which was Simon Jubeba?

During the trial's eleven weeks – spread over two years – only three witnesses had mentioned the two men by name.

The others had simply referred to "the shorter one", or "the deceased", or "the longer man". The new defence team had shown no more inclination towards clarifying the matter than their predecessors had. It was the state's case, and the state's problem. But in fact the prosecution seemed equally confused. This was obvious in that their final written arguments to the judge opened with a sentence that had the men's surnames the wrong way round.

It was the recent testimony of Professor Jan Botha that had finally brought the matter into sharp focus – twice – and had led the judge to calling Samuel's mother and Simon's aunts to the witness stand.

During his testimony the forensic expert had roundly denounced the staff at Parys Hospital for somehow managing to give Samuel, on admission, an "inexplicable" Glasgow Coma Scale reading of fourteen over fifteen. "I don't think any reasonably experienced medical officer could make such a mistake," Botha had said. He had studied the photos of the autopsy, he said, and the gaping fracture wound in the deceased's skull, and it was clear to him that the G.C.S. reading was wrong. The only other possibility – one that Kobus Burger had endorsed early on – was that something had happened to Samuel overnight in hospital. A "subsequent injury". Perhaps he'd slipped off his bed. Or a heavy piece of medical equipment had fallen on his head. The professor had seen such things happen before.

State prosecutor J.J. Mlotshwa interrupted this chain of thought. "Perhaps we are talking about a different deceased," he interjected gently.

"No – I don't understand," Botha replied in a sharp tone.

In this instance, however, the prosecutor was right. The defence's key forensic witness, a professor with an eight-page resume, had been reading the wrong autopsy report. He'd been reading the autopsy report for Simon Jubeba, not Samuel Tjixa.

He had got the bodies mixed up.

Directed towards the correct report, he changed his mind and concluded that it was perfectly possible that Samuel, with a policeman at his bedside overnight, had been correctly diagnosed on admission and had been suffering from a progressive head injury.

"So, the death of the deceased five hours later would not surprise you?" Mlotshwa now asked.

"Correct," the professor said, curtly.

The second and more significant confusion concerned Simon's body, or more specifically, his skull. When Simon had arrived by ambulance, barely alive, in Bloemfontein, the trauma doctor in the Casualty department, Van Tonder, who had been expecting him for hours, had noted that his patient had a catastrophic skull fracture. He'd pressed on his right forehead and felt a queasy, unnatural softness. There was no mistaking it.

But days later, when it was time for Simon's autopsy, Dr Lairi had not only missed the injury, but had subsequently gone out of his way to tell the court that "there was no skull fracture".

It was possible that Lairi had simply missed it. His autopsy report had, after all, been condemned as almost amateur. But there was another theory that Van Tonder couldn't rule out, and nor could Professor Botha. This was that somewhere between Pelonomi Hospital in Bloemfontein and the city's morgue there could have been a mix-up. Perhaps Lairi had done his autopsy on the wrong body ...

"This is bizarre. I really cannot explain how this came about, My Lady. It is almost inexplicable," Professor Botha told the court.

"Will you agree there is a big possibility — may I say probability, in fact — that the patient admitted to hospital was not the same person on whom the post-mortem was conducted?" Botha was asked by the defence.

"I wondered about the identity of the person with the skull injury ... I really cannot explain it," he replied. Dr Lairi's failure to mention the fracture in his post-mortem report "made me wonder if this was the right body."

The defence team was delighted. Surely this proved there was reasonable doubt about the credibility of Simon's autopsy. A convenient cloud of confusion had enveloped the whole case. The chain of medical evidence had been broken. Add that to the whole issue of the injuries that Simon and Samuel might well have sustained while they were being driven over rough ground in the back of a police van — the "novus actus" that Kobus Burger had latched onto at the start of the trial — and suddenly the state's case was crumbling. How could the prosecution argue that the accused had murdered anyone when they couldn't even be sure they had the right bodies, or the right injuries?

"A soldier is only as good as his weapon," said the most

senior defence lawyer, Piet Pistorius, gesturing towards the prosecution. "In this case I submit they have no weapon."

*

In the witness box, Ruth studied the photographs. Earlier, sitting on the bench behind Rikki and Gusta, she'd asked the man beside her if her son would be wearing clothes in the pictures she would be shown.

"I'm very sorry to have to do this," the judge said, after first apologising for being unable to pronounce Ruth's surname, Qokotha.

Ruth initially seemed dazed. As if the event was simply overwhelming.

"Yes. It is my son," she said quietly, as she was shown a photograph, taken from the side, of Samuel lying, shirtless, on a hospital bed in Parys with blood covering the left side of his face. The next photograph was from the morgue – a close-up of Samuel's head, looking cold, bruised, and shiny under a harsh light, as he lay on a metal gurney.

"It is my son," Ruth said. She slumped forward, head down.

But the judge had more questions. She wanted to know if Ruth knew the other deceased.

Of course she did.

Whether she'd read the form she'd signed at the morgue in Sasolburg.

No, she hadn't read the form – she'd been too confused.

Which parts of Samuel's body had Ruth actually seen at the morgue?

Just his face.

Had Ruth seen a label on him?

No.

The judge insisted that her questions were necessary, that they were "in the interests of justice".

But the truth was more mundane. There was, and had never been, any uncertainty about Unknown Male Two. No broken chain of evidence. No mystery. He had been Samuel Tjixa all along.

It was Simon's skull fracture that had caused doubt. His two aunts quickly identified the photographs of his body – taken at various stages in Bloemfontein – as being Simon.

Perhaps the hospital had got his X-rays mixed up. Perhaps Dr Lairi had just overlooked the skull fracture. That would be for the judge to decide. In the meantime, Ruth had been summoned to court, three years after her son's death, simply because nobody there had taken the trouble to check their notes.

Now she was being shown a copy of Samuel's death certificate and asked if she recognised it, and what it meant, and whether she understood the phrase "unnatural death".

Ruth had had enough. She didn't understand the phrase. Instead of replying, she began to stamp her left foot, in mute fury, on the wooden floor.

"Would you like to take a break? Perhaps five minutes to drink some water?" the judge asked her, as Ruth's shoulders shook and her head slumped lower.

An hour later, on the way home, she would make a joke about what happened next. Like she always did. Eish! Did you hear what I told her? But at the time she could not contain her rage anymore.

"No, I don't want to take a break," she half shouted. "I just want this to be finished. I just want to be left alone, to say nothing more. My son is dead. There is nothing more I can do."

28

A COMMON PURPOSE

THE TRIAL ENDED a few minutes later. In her closing
remarks, the judge warned those present not to expect a
speedy verdict. After all, it had been a staggeringly complicated case and she would need several months to sift through
the evidence and the relevant legal principles. It was agreed
that she would only hand down her verdict at the end of
May 2019, just within the officially stipulated three-month
period.

But on the weekend before the court was due to reconvene,
the judge announced that she was sick. Two months later she
postponed again, with a day's notice. A new date was set in
October 2019.

Shortly before 6.00 p.m. on an orange-skied evening,
the day before the verdict would finally be read, Rikki van
der Westhuizen walked through the side door of the Dutch
Reformed Church and headed over to a pew on the far side,
her head fizzing with thoughts.

"Do not be dismayed, for I am your God. I will strengthen
you and help you. I will uphold you with my righteous right
hand."

Inside the darkening church Dominee Ian Jonker read out

a few verses from the Book of Isaiah in his gruff, measured voice. Blocks of evening sunlight fell on the wall behind him.

Rikki, straight-backed, turned to glance at Boeta, seated beside her now, grimy from the fields, still wearing his shorts and work boots, and she asked herself, not for the first time, who was this dour, difficult man she'd married?

In recent weeks Boeta had almost stopped sleeping. She would hear him moving around the house at night, ox-like, looking for something to eat, turning on the television, phoning Anton for another long chat. At least he was taking his drugs now that she was back home with the family. Rikki would hear the T.V. go on and then she'd sink into a deep sleep, buffeted by vivid dreams about the verdict – about visiting her husband in prison after he'd been sentenced to life for murder.

Rikki's mother, Sheila, was Scottish. A born teacher, people always said. Sheila had been a patient woman – like her daughter – whose parents had emigrated from Britain before she was born. Later she had married an Afrikaans man she'd met while studying at the University of the Free State.

Thank God, Rikki thought, neither of her parents was still alive to see this.

Rikki had never pictured herself living out on the farms. In her early twenties, she'd been a social worker, travelling into the black townships, dealing with child welfare, foster parents, neglect, abuse. She'd loved it. But she'd already met Boeta at high school and, despite her family's quiet misgivings, had found herself drawn into the whole farming world – the thrill of the harvests, the rugby, the giant tractors, the noisy Van der Westhuizen clan – and suddenly she was married, then pregnant, and her career in social work fell away.

"All my ambition … I surrender it into your hands," Rikki sang now, quietly, reading the hymn's lyrics as they were projected onto the wall.

Dominee Jonker had arranged a special service, just for the six accused and their immediate families. Rikki and Boeta sat alone. On purpose, it seemed. Across the aisle, Anton and Gusta sat near their son Cor. Captain Prinsloo had come with his wife, a daughter and his parents. Miela and Crista sat at the back with their baby daughter. Of the accused, only Klein Loedie, Rikki and Boeta's son, was absent – it seemed he didn't approve of the church's liberal attitude to things like gay marriage, and preferred to keep himself busy with the cattle, still hardly talking to his parents.

After all the torment of the past few years, Rikki was surprised to find she could now contemplate Boeta with a degree of detachment. As if she were an outsider – which perhaps she was. It reminded her of the neutral, professional way she used to assess the poor souls who shuffled along the corridors at work. She could look back and see the warning signs, the things she'd missed, or chosen not to see, in her own household, in her husband, in her youngest daughter too. The guilt she felt about Marie, lying there on her bedroom floor, could still grab her, like a hand on her throat.

It was money and shame that had first broken Boeta, Rikki now understood. Fifteen years ago, when their farm had sunk into debt and he'd had to drive across the fields to visit his father, to ask for a bailout, and to listen to the old man's gruff "told you so" lectures. That was when it had all started to go wrong. As much as he'd railed against his father, he'd always wanted to impress him too. The spark, the clumsy energy that Rikki had cherished in Boeta never properly recovered from that. He drank more. He suffered bouts of depression. He took it out on his workers and on his family.

She didn't like to think of her husband as a violent man. But it was true.

It had become true.

Then came that long evening in January 2016. Rikki had never warmed to her father-in-law. To Oom Loedie. That old-fashioned sternness – the cruelty of it. She had kept her distance from him over the years. But she could see it from Boeta's point of view too. She would have reacted the same way, with the same fury, if her own parents had been attacked by thieves.

I would have gone ballistic, she said. When it's your own father, your grandfather, it's not like it's the neighbours. How could anyone keep their cool?

Still, she knew Boeta was a special case.

It was like expecting a man in a wheelchair to walk – that's how she thought of it now. He can't walk. He just can't. Boeta lacked the skills to deal with the situation in that field just as he struggled with its long, drawn-out aftermath. Which is why he didn't take his pills, why he lashed out at the Hawks, why he needed her back at the house, despite everything, to keep him and his family in some sort of order.

Dominee Jonker interrupted her train of thought.

"Truly He is my rock and my salvation; He is my fortress, I will not be shaken," he read from the Book of Psalms.

What would they all have done without Dominee Jonker? Short, solid, unflappable and patient. That first evening, after the attack, he'd rushed out to sit and pray with Oom Loedie. Soon after, the dominee had been the one to calm tensions ahead of the bail hearing, summoning people to the Parys aerodrome to pray, persuading most of the white right-wingers who'd come from out of town, looking for trouble, to put their guns back in their cars and drive home. Let the law take its course, he'd urged them.

On Sundays, Rikki preferred to sit upstairs in church — away from the crowds that squeezed into every last pew. She knew that the congregation, indeed the whole town, gossiped about Boeta. About the way his father's money had always got him out of trouble, out of debt, out of custody, even that time as a youngster when he'd shot a zebra by the side of the road. Or when he'd been driving drunk and hit that woman, and had got away with paying a fine on both counts. And who knew, they muttered, what had really happened that day on the farm. Maybe the two black men had come to Boeta first to ask for money, and maybe he'd given them the gun and told them to rob his father, told them to kill him so he could get the inheritance. And what was the plan for the two thieves, dumped in the back of that bakkie after they'd been beaten up? Were Boeta and Anton, realising the two were badly injured, planning to drive them into the bush before the police arrived, in order to bury the bodies or to pretend they'd jumped off the back trying to escape and had killed themselves?

It seemed all too possible, people said.

Then there was the other sort of chatter. The wishful thinking kind. What if Captain Prinsloo hadn't got lost on the way to the scene that evening, and had arrived in time to stop the worst of the assaults? What if the fathers of those young Van der Westhuizens – Muller and his friends – had not gone away on holiday over the New Year? Surely, they would have reined in their boys? And what if they'd found that missing gun? They could have proved to the Hawks that it was a farm robbery, that their anger was justified, that this was all just a case of a legitimate arrest that had got a little out of hand in a country where farmers had every reason to feel under threat.

Another white farmer had recently been killed in the neighbourhood. The *Parys Gazette* described Theunis Bosch as the 24th local victim of a farm murder. The 74-year-old had been shot with his own pistol inside his house on the edge of the nearby town of Vredefort, and was found lying in a pool of blood, surrounded by signs of a violent struggle.

"Another and another," fumed Gusta Loggenberg.

Anton's wife waved her fury like a flag these days. She had taken to circulating gruesome photos of the victims on social media, sharing her indignation with a wider group of whites who muttered, online, about the good old days in Rhodesia and clamoured for the world to acknowledge a genocide being waged against white farmers. Why did people only make a fuss when blacks were being killed?

After that last attack, Pieter Kemp, the bearded ex-soldier who helped co-ordinate security on the farms, had sent out his own WhatsApp message.

"We need to look out for the old people who live alone on farms. Please send names and pin-drops of where the elderly in your area live."

But Kemp had no time for talk of a genocide. No, no, no. Not for a moment. He shook his head. That kind of language was just being used to excite people, to stir up the right-wingers, to excite the sort of fools who'd come to town three years back looking for trouble during those early bail hearings, waving their old flags, clutching their rifles, and spoiling for a fight. The truth was simple – the farmers had guns and cash, and everyone knew it, and so they were tempting targets, white or black. Kemp didn't even like the term "farm attack". It was just robbery, or violent robbery. Why politicise everything? Kemp had once gone to complain to the local police about the lack of security on the farms but the commander had shown him the statistics – two or three murders every month in the township and maybe six reported rapes.

So where would you put your manpower? the commander had asked Kemp, who realised he had no answer.

The service was nearly over now. The orange glow inside the church was turning to gloom. Rikki glanced across at Gusta and Anton, sitting close together, their backs straight, chins jutting forward. How had Gusta put up with him, she wondered? Boeta might have his violent moments, but Anton ...

Rikki shuddered, reached for her handbag, and got to her feet. A line popped into her head, something she'd heard before her marriage, a phrase that had often floated into her thoughts, unbidden, since then – not least when she thought of Anton, or of some other neighbours, or those 204s, those boys – men now – who would surely be haunted for ever by what they'd done, whatever the outcome of the trial. These are not gentle people, she said to herself.

*

The next morning, the court reconvened and Judge Corné van Zyl began reading out parts of her verdict. But it soon became apparent that there was no end in sight. Somehow, over the four days set aside for the verdict to be delivered, the judge contrived to use only four hours of court time. It seemed clear that she had still not finished writing her judgment.

The lawyers shrugged. Everyone else sighed. Another date would have to be set and a new decade would begin before the accused would take their positions and hear the judge's decision.

*

Friday May 8, 2020, was a cold, clear day. Winter had begun to settle on the fields around Parys after a strong harvest.

In the magistrate's court Judge Corné van Zyl paused for perhaps thirty seconds, frowned, and flipped between the pages of a notebook that lay, filled with her handwriting and marked with a dozen small pink Post-it notes, on the large and cluttered desk before her. The judge had been addressing the accused for almost an hour, and it now seemed clear that she was poised to deliver her verdict to a silent courtroom.

"This trial was, to say the least, very challenging," she declared in her gentle voice. "There have been a lot of hiccups."

Ruth had left the court a few minutes earlier, shaking her head, not trusting her emotions. Inexplicably, the Jubebas – Simon's family – had not shown up at all today. But the six accused and their relatives now peered, insistently, at the judge from behind their face masks.

Curiously, it was the arrival of Covid-19 that had finally compelled the judge towards this moment, a year and two months after the trial itself had ended. The virus had initially provided an opportunity for more court postponements, but eventually this date in court held. Because of the government's lockdown rules, however, Judge van Zyl was obliged to issue only a brief summary verdict, rather than a full and lengthy judgment, on account of the danger of exposing people to the virus for too long in an open court.

And so the six accused now sat a yard apart, on a long bench in Parys' largest courtroom, listening to the judge's opening remarks. The atmosphere was oddly muted at first. A handful of relatives were spread out across the other benches. No other spectators. With the lockdown still in force and the rest of the courthouse silent today, it felt almost like people were attending school on a weekend or a public holiday.

The judge had begun by rattling through the testimony of the 204 witnesses – sketching out a verbal diagram that indicated who had, allegedly, hit whom with what, according to Wian, or Wicus or Fanie or the others.

Next, she'd confronted the issue that had somehow eluded

all three of them – the prosecution, defence and judge – throughout the trial: precisely which deceased was which. Which man was Simon, which was Samuel?

"I accept," she'd declared, her voice muffled by her own black mask, "that the shorter one was Samuel" and the taller one, necessarily, was Simon.

She had got that bit right. But then she sought to apply that new distinction to the crime scene itself, and soon veered off course. She stated that the man lying on his back in Anton Loggenberg's bakkie – the man allegedly whipped and electrocuted and told to "Die, dog, die" – had been Samuel. She was wrong.

Below her, at the front of the court, prosecutor J.J. Mlotshwa sat hunched over, almost out of the judge's line of sight, his head bent towards his knees. Earlier, in the sunshine outside, he had told people that he would get at least two murder convictions today, and culpable homicide for the rest of them. That was the bare minimum. Now he listened to the judge as she began to dissect, to weigh up, the strength of the state's case, starting at its core, with the evidence of the 204s.

On face value, she said, their statements appeared to be similar. But on closer inspection it was clear that there were not only huge differences, but contradictions, and worse. In fact, there appeared to be what she called a "golden thread" running through all of their evidence – namely, an attempt to downplay the seriousness of the witnesses' own assaults while exaggerating those of the accused. As for the idea that the 204s were merely "boasting" when they had confessed to so many violent acts on those curse-filled voice notes, the judge was not convinced.

It had remained the prosecution's strangest gamble. Why offer a deal to so many prospective 204s? Sons, nephews, a farm manager, his brother and son. Why not just take one of them as a state witness? Or better still, put them all on trial and leave the judge to make sense of the whole mess. Now the prosecution's gamble appeared to be failing.

Mlotshwa's head seemed to dip another inch.

The judge continued, fast, like a teacher trying to finish a lesson before the bell rings.

There was the manner in which the 204s' statements had been taken by the Hawks. The witnesses had given different versions of the process, and of the involvement of multiple lawyers. The judge hastened to point out that she wasn't questioning the integrity of Oscar Pistorius' famous defence lawyer, Barry Roux, who had been hired by Vicky van der Westhuizen to oversee a potential 204 deal with the prosecution for his closest relatives and farmworkers. But still, she announced, the way those statements were taken by the Hawks was definitely "not in the interests of justice" or "of the truth".

Another serious blow for the state.

"So pathetic," one of the Hawks officers reacted, angrily, under his breath.

The judge was implying that she believed the defence claims of some sort of corrupt stitch-up by the police in terms of the 204s' evidence – the heart of the prosecution's case.

And it got worse.

A year earlier, Mlotshwa had conceded in his closing

arguments that there was no hard evidence of "dolus directus" – direct intention – when it came to the two murders. In other words, the state could not prove that the farmers had set out that evening with the intention of killing Simon or Samuel. But the prosecution had insisted it had shown the men were guilty of murder in terms of "dolus eventualis" – in that they could and should have foreseen (like Oscar Pistorius shooting through that bathroom door) that their violent actions might lead to the men's deaths, and that the legal doctrine of common purpose, of being engaged in a joint endeavour, should also apply in this case and to the charges of murder.

It was this common purpose argument that still fuelled Mlotshwa's confidence in securing culpable homicide convictions. After all, the farmers had watched each other take turns assaulting the two men. None had physically intervened to stop the violence. They must have understood, and reconciled themselves with the fact, that such injuries – head injuries, in particular – might lead to death. It surely didn't matter who had done exactly what, and to whom. It was a collective assault that had led to the men's deaths.

But now, in her summary judgment, Van Zyl spent all of ten seconds dismissing that argument out of hand and without explanation. The state had simply "failed to prove common purpose between the respective accused".

Mlotshwa blinked hard and turned to look at his colleagues.

There was something about the brevity of the summary judgment that gave every word an extra punch. And the implications for the prosecution were now surfacing, like a pattern of dark, fresh bruises. If common purpose had been rejected, then everything now hung on the strength of the cases the state had built against each accused, and on the chain of evidence that linked the men's individual actions to Simon and Samuel's specific injuries. Anton standing on Samuel's head. Boeta hitting Simon's face with a gun. And so on.

"There are serious shortcomings in the so-called chain of evidence presented by the state."

The judge ploughed on. The defence lawyers' heads nodded sharply over their legal pads, like a row of pecking hens.

And it was true. From the police docket through to closing arguments, the prosecution had never shown a real inclination to match any particular post-mortem wound to any actions by the accused. They'd been preoccupied by a simpler equation – of a collective beating equalling two dead men. And now, to back up her conclusion, the judge turned to the evidence of Professor Jan Botha, the defence's star witness – the retired forensic pathologist who had been so critical of the post-mortems that he'd even wondered if they'd been carried out on the right bodies.

Professor Botha's testimony, it quickly became clear, had carried huge weight with the judge, who now endorsed his startling claim that "none of the injuries" suffered by the deceased could have caused their deaths.

*

If there had been crowds outside the courthouse that morning, as there had been in the early days of the case, it is easy to imagine that now might have been the time for the protest songs to start, as news of the judge's forceful opinions began to filter out. The nationwide lockdown partly explained why Philip Street was so quiet today. But that wasn't the only factor. This case had been going on for four years now. Other cases, other news, had intruded. South Africa's television and radio news stations and its major newspapers had lost all interest in the case some time ago and had sent no cameras to cover the verdict. Many people in Parys, weary of the endless postponements, had detached themselves in a similar fashion.

At this point the judge was still flipping between her notes, to the evident frustration of Mlotshwa, who seemed convinced that she had not actually written her full judgment yet and was therefore offering, not a summary, but a scattergun series of observations, like a student trying to bluff her way through a classroom presentation. But the prosecution had more pressing concerns. Its case was collapsing. It was now left with one last hope.

A year earlier, Mlotshwa had urged the judge, with some emotion, to remember how badly injured Simon and Samuel had been shown to be before they were loaded into the police van. They had – it was surely not in dispute – been beaten unconscious by the farmers. The state pathologist who had conducted the post-mortems had been clear on that too – and angrily so, lashing out at the defence lawyer who had suggested that the two men might have died from injuries suffered as they lay in the police van as it crossed a bumpy field, bitterly reminding a hushed courtroom of the case of Steve Biko. Whatever subsequent injuries they might have suffered in the van could, surely, only be a result of them having been already so badly hurt that they could no longer protect themselves.

Now it was the judge's turn to decide whether the state was right – whether it was beyond reasonable doubt that Simon and Samuel had been killed by the farmers' fists, gun and boots, or whether a "novus actus interveniens", a new act, in the form of a rough field and the hard metal of a van's corrugated floor, had intervened to break that chain of evidence.

*

Captain Henk Prinsloo had been waiting his turn in the dock, occasionally looking back over his shoulder towards his wife, Rona. Four wasted years, he thought. His career and finances in ruins. But the girls had come through it, the family had come through it together, maybe even stronger now. His mind drifted to his police ID papers, his firearm and cellphone, still sitting in a safe at the police station next door. Yes, that would be his first step, to collect his gun, to put the bitterness behind him, and become not just a free man, but a proper policeman again. He might always hold a grudge against Captain Laux and his Hawks team, but they were the ones who would have to live with the way they'd treated him.

In front of Prinsloo, the judge was now racing through her notes. The evidence of all three state witnesses who had implicated the policeman, accusing him of using a cattle-prod to shock Simon's genitals, was "to be rejected", she said. At those words, Rona's shoulders began to shake.

"I find that the version of accused number 3 is reasonably,

possibly true," the judge went on. Poking someone in the ribs with a torch can constitute assault, but not in these circumstances. In fact, she said, Captain Prinsloo, cleared now of all wrongdoing, could even leave the dock, separating himself at last from the company of the other five accused, and move to the back of the court to comfort his wife.

*

Now came the state's last stand. Its last remaining argument. Two black men had been caught and beaten and killed by a group of farmers. However hard it was to apportion individual blame, and regardless of what had happened to Simon and Samuel after they had left the field – the van ride, any misdiagnosis in Parys hospital, Simon's slow ambulance journey to Bloemfontein, and the confusion that had subsequently enveloped their bodies and post-mortems – surely the judge would, at the very least, acknowledge that.

Judge van Zyl glanced up from her notes, then turned once again to Professor Botha's evidence. She quoted his conclusion that both Simon and Samuel "could have sustained serious injuries or could have suffered from aggravation of injuries during the transport in the back of the police van". Then she noted that the professor had also testified that "both deceased could have died as a result of improper medical assistance".

And that was that. Reasonable doubt.

The accused were asked to stand. The judge declared that the professor's evidence had "upset" the state's entire case against them, and had led her to accept the possibility – or even the probability – that one or more "novus actus", either in the police van, or the hospital, or both, had intervened to cause, or contribute to, Simon and Samuel's deaths. As a result, she could not convict Boeta van der Westhuizen, Anton Loggenberg, Cor Loggenberg, Loedie van der Westhuizen or Miela Janse van Rensburg on the basis of the state's case. Professor Botha's testimony had been decisive.

"I am convinced," she said, "that the state did not prove the counts of murder, nor the competent verdict of manslaughter – culpable homicide."

A few minutes later, as the men shuffled along the bench to leave the courtroom, Mlotshwa turned to his colleagues. Twenty years earlier he'd been struck off the roll, barred from being a lawyer for five years following allegations of impropriety. He'd fought his way back to become one of the top prosecutors in the country. He would not take this new defeat lying down either. The state would appeal this pathetic joke of a verdict. Of course it would. There was a mountain of case law to back it up on the "novus actus" ruling and on common purpose too. This was not the end of the matter.

The defence team had still been scribbling away as the judge read out her verdicts.

Not guilty of murder.

Not guilty of murder.

Five times over.

But all five farmers were found guilty of assault. And not just common assault, but assault with intention to do grievous bodily harm. They would remain free on bail until late August, when they'd be sentenced. Klein Loedie had also been found guilty of destroying evidence by burning his friends' blood-stained shoes and the fan-belt used to whip Simon. But their lawyers had no concerns about any custodial sentences. None at all. Not after the judge had rejected the state's entire case. Not after four years of financial and emotional trauma. There was absolutely no risk, they were confident, of a single one of their clients spending a day in prison.

The 204s had not been in court today. A year earlier the defence advocate had contemptuously dismissed the accused's relatives as liars and told the judge he would relish the day when Muller, Wian, Wicus, Fanie, Johann and Daniel faced prosecution for murder. But the judge had not yet made a final ruling on whether they'd done enough in the witness stand to secure immunity, and the general feeling around court was that the prosecution would be highly unlikely to pursue them anyway.

A scrum now formed at the courtroom door. Boeta and Anton hugged their wives and clapped their lawyers on the back. To hell with social distancing. The whole crowd of them made their way into the sky-lit lobby, a ripple of unleashed energy suddenly dancing through their bodies, and only the crinkles at the corners of their eyes giving any hint of the emotions playing across their masked faces.

In her usual spot in the shade, Ruth watched the farmers emerge from the courthouse. Free men. She had not expected that. And yes, of course, if pressed, she would admit to feeling angry, outraged. But in that instant – as the farmers strolled past her – she felt distracted by a more pressing concern.

All these years she'd waited, hoping that those who, she believed, had killed Samuel would somehow step in, financially, to fill the gap he'd left in her life – would build her a home, somewhere proper, somewhere that didn't flood when the rains came. Now that seemed unlikely. She was fifty-eight. Two more years before she could get her pension. She'd asked, three times, for state aid because of her ill health. No luck.

A Hawks officer agreed to give Ruth a lift back to her shack in his car. But she knew he would probably take her only as far as Sasolburg and then tell her to catch a minibus taxi. Another R12 that she didn't have. Eish.

EPILOGUE

I T WAS THE first time Samuel's brother, Elias, had been back to the cemetery since the burials – a hot summer afternoon with birdsong on the edge of Tumahole, rain clouds drifting away to the west, and a dozen nonchalant brown cows mooing to each other as they jostled their way across the slope above the graves.

Over the years Elias had talked, often, about buying a headstone for his brother, and now that he had the job at the abattoir, perhaps that would soon be possible. He needed to start saving but he had too many responsibilities – two children with different mothers, one of whom was fighting him in the courts for maintenance; Lawrence still without a job, and now his mother's troubles. Ruth had been drinking too much recently, spending the weekends propped against the side of their shack, legs stretched out in front of her like tree roots, bloodshot eyes and a glazed smile, saying sorry, sorry, to anyone and everyone, the neighbours tutting, but let them.

A few weeks back, someone found Ruth in the field behind their shack. She had gone out looking for wild spinach, or something similar, to cook for her boys, had suddenly felt dizzy. She woke up hours later with a stranger shaking her, asking what was wrong.

Ruth swore she would never drink again. But she felt tired all the time. Too tired. The H.I.V. was part of the problem – she had found out she was carrying the virus a few months after her husband Elias died. Even her memories of him were souring. She had laughed about her husband's drinking before, but now she remembered the harder times, all those women, the way he barely even tried to hide his infidelities, and that time one of them had come over to confront her and they'd fought – the girl had stuck a knife in her back, but she'd grabbed her in a headlock and wrestled her to the ground all the same. Hah!

Just the other day she'd shocked her sons, praying in front of them on the linoleum floor in the shack one night, asking God to "take me now". You mustn't talk like that, they told her sternly. When she spoke about it later, she turned it into a joke, as she still did with difficult things. A grumpy old widow talking nonsense, looking for a laugh at her own expense. But sometimes it wasn't a joke. Sometimes she just felt like she wanted everything to end.

Her sons' visit to the graves was a spur-of-the-moment thing. Elias and Lawrence had caught a lift to Tumahole and were passing by Simon's old house. Elias went in to greet the Jubeba family – two of Simon's sisters, Dimakatso and Jemina, were at home – and suggested they go to the grave-yard together, partly because it seemed right and partly because neither Elias nor Lawrence could remember exactly how to get there, all the way across the township. Lawrence has chosen to wait silently outside the house. He didn't have much time for the Jubebas. They were like children, always squabbling, always some new problem.

Eventually, the four of them set off – five including Dimakatso's baby, asleep on her back – hitching a ride down the hill past the stadium, past the corner where the minibus taxis gathered, and on, out beyond the ostrich farm and past the iron gates of the old cemetery with its tree-lined avenues and marbled rows.

"For the whites," said Elias, nodding towards the trees, as the car swung sharply to the left and headed back up the hill.

*

Dimakatso's thoughts drifted back to January 2016, and not just to Simon and Samuel.

There had been a third man.

His name was Baba. Baba Mbele. He'd been friends with the other two for years, drinking with them, making wild plans, chasing girls in the township. Three bosom friends, some said. But Baba had been in jail a few times and had a reputation for using a knife in fights and for being rough with women. Rougher than usual. Dimakatso had seen enough of him over the years – out late in the shebeens, drunk and much too insistent with her friends – to know him to be a bad person.

Still, in the first days of 2016, Baba had seemed to be the only one with a plan. A way to make some cash. He told Simon and Samuel that he'd found work for the three of them – a tiling job – in Sasolburg. Dimakatso had heard them discussing it, like excited kids, making plans for how they'd spend the money they'd earn. Simon was going to fix the window he'd broken at home, and help pay for another ceremony to mark their mother's death. A few days earlier he'd been to the Labour Department to see about getting unemployment benefit, after that Boeta van der Westhuizen had chased him off his farm for stealing sausages. He'd even called Boeta to ask him to sign the papers and Boeta had screamed down the phone at him, threatening to kill him if he ever saw him again. But Simon wouldn't let it go. In fact, he told the others, they could stop off at Boeta's farm on their way to the new job in Sasolburg – then he'd have to sign the forms.

Simon had been a fast sprinter as a child but had injured his knee playing football. His limp came back after the last beating Boeta had given him over the sausages. It was another reason to resent the Van der Westhuizens.

On the morning of Wednesday, January 6, 2016, Simon, Samuel and Baba caught a lift and set off for Sasolburg. On the way, Simon called his sister Jemina, who was living there, to tell her he was on the way and wanted to meet up to make arrangements for their mother's ceremony. He mentioned the business with Boeta, about how he was going to get the money for the ceremony from him.

A few hours later Jemina tried calling Simon back on his phone but it was switched off. She tried Samuel's number. Same thing. She didn't have Baba's number, but Dimakatso did and she tried but couldn't get through.

Late the next evening, Jemina ran into Baba in Zamdela, Sasolburg's township. By then everyone had heard about the incident and what had happened to Simon and Samuel and the rumour that there were three people involved. "Two blacks, or maybe three," as old man Loedie van der Westhuizen had first said to Boeta on the phone.

Jemina asked Baba, straight out, what had happened.

No, I didn't go with them to the farm. I don't even know what happened, Baba told her. The last time I saw them both was in Parys.

Jemina looked at Baba's right leg. It was covered in some sort of bandage. He wouldn't say what had happened to it and when Jemina – not even trying to hide her scepticism – started asking more questions, he took off, limping away into the night.

A month later, in February, Baba turned up at Simon's family home in Tumahole.

The two families, the Mbeles and the Jubebas, were neighbours in the township and had been close for decades, but since the killings things had turned sour. The first proper sign of trouble had come at Simon's funeral, which the Mbeles conspicuously failed to attend. A couple of weeks after that the Mbele family sent a delegation down the street to complain about witchcraft. According to Dimakatso, the family said they had been afraid to come to the funeral in case they were attacked. And then Baba had fallen ill. The Mbeles had concluded that the Jubebas had cast some sort of spell over them, as punishment for the fact that Simon had died. All this was muttered behind closed doors.

When Baba turned up at the Jubebas' house, Dimakatso, heavily pregnant, was standing in the doorway. He said nothing, just forced his way past her, a strange, intense look on his face. Inside, he turned to the left, strode two paces over to the wall behind one of the sofas, and took down a photograph of Simon – a life-sized, blurry headshot in a new black and gold frame. He held it carefully in both hands and then turned, walked back outside and stood by the thin wire fence, still staring at the picture. Dimakatso, from her position in the doorway, watched him as he briefly tucked the frame under his arm to light a cigarette. He took a long drag on it, and then, in a gesture of gentleness and intimacy, held the burning cigarette in front of Simon's two-dimensional mouth. There was a pause. Baba took another drag and did the same thing again.

What are you doing? Dimakatso asked.

I heard about what happened, about how things turned out, he replied.

So what really did happen that day?

I'm not ready to talk now. But when I'm ready, I'll talk.

And suddenly Baba was on his knees, sobbing hard, trying to talk but making no sense.

Dimakatso stared at him for a moment, felt a brief twinge of sympathy, and then felt it drain away. She told him to leave, to get the hell out of her family's home.

I'm not going anywhere.

She took out her phone and said she would call the police – right then. Baba looked up at her, put the photograph on the ground and stood up. Then he walked out onto the dirt road. Dimakatso never saw him again.

Indeed, for the longest time no-one seemed to speak of

Baba much at all. It was almost like a collective secret. Easier – for his friends, and perhaps for the farmers and the police too – to forget about a third man who had somehow escaped, unseen, across the dry fields. And then, about two years later, his death was announced in Tumahole. He was thirty-four. Dimakatso, who'd once stumbled on some pills in his lunchbox when she'd been pregnant and hungry and rooting around for food, thought she knew what had killed him, but nothing was said in public. Instead he was buried a little way up the hill from Simon and Samuel. Dimakatso and the rest of the Jubeba family chose not to attend the funeral.

*

There was a fence, of sorts, around the new municipal cemetery. Elias, Dimakatso and the others got out of the car and walked, in a group at first, over the rough terrain. It had rained heavily in the past few days, the water rippling down the hillside and cutting small gullies into the red earth. In the top corner, three deep graves had recently been dug, close together, ready for Saturday's funerals. Beyond them, the rest were laid out, more or less chronologically, in lines that snaked across the contours of the hill, descending towards the oldest graves – dating back to 2010 – on the bottom row. A whole hillside covered in under a decade.

Dimakatso and her family had not been in court to hear the judge deliver her verdicts on the white farmers. Not for lack of interest, or for fear – like Ruth – of being too overwhelmed by the moment. It was simply that no-one at the courthouse, or the police station, or anyone in the prosecution team, had bothered to let them know it was even happening. When she'd been told about the outcome a few hours later, Dimakatso had let out a short, hollow laugh and sunk onto the sofa, staring at the floor. My phone was on – they had my number, she'd said. So how did the farmers react? Were they smiling beneath those masks? The verdicts felt so wrong. But how to make them right, and where to even start? Not for the first time, she'd felt a numbing chill of powerlessness.

"Over here?" Elias called out, hesitantly, after few minutes.

There had to be a thousand graves here by now. A handful had proper headstones carved with words about remembrance and love. Some were marked by breezeblocks, each with a yellow painted number. There was a large concrete cross, a scattering of plastic flowers, and lots of old glass bottles and cans pushed into the mounds.

Elias thought he might have found the right row. There was a headstone with 2016 on it. He worked his way along, trying to find the graves for January, thinking about Samuel's funeral – about how many shovels of earth he'd put onto the coffin – and trying not to trip. There were a few big mounds, but most had been swept away by the rains, and in a few graves the ground itself had settled dramatically, dropping a foot or more to reveal the old, sharp edges carved out by the digger.

The others headed over to where Elias was standing, stepping over weeds and gullies, looking for clues. But there were no more clues. The rain had ripped through this part of the cemetery, burying several breezeblocks and upending even some of the bigger headstones. Dimakatso gave a soft sigh. A few seconds later Elias shrugged. He turned and walked back to the car. Such was life, they both seemed to be saying. No sense in complaining. Besides, who would listen? Perhaps he'd come back another time, Elias said – maybe with Ruth. She would want to tidy things up.

With everyone back in the car and the doors closed, they cautiously backed out of the empty cemetery. To the north, the crescent of hills had turned green again – blue green, like a long, unbroken, ancient wave rolling in gently across the high, endless plains.

AUTHOR'S NOTE

I T'S A BRIGHT day in the tree-lined yard outside the Parys magistrate's court, and I'm doing something that has become a routine over the course of the past few years. First, I sit on the low wall beneath the tree with Ruth and Selina — mother and aunt of the two dead men. A few minutes later, I stroll over to the prosecution, who usually stand further to the left, near the water tap, in dark suits and immaculately polished shoes. After that, I join the defence lawyers and their clients sitting on the wall on the right-hand side of the court-yard, invariably sharing biltong or sandwiches. And then I walk towards the gate that leads through to the police station. This is where the Hawks stand, smoking, in a huddle, some-times with one or two of their 204 witnesses. If there's time before the trial resumes, I chat to the translator or to the local journalists and unfailingly cheerful court officials.

It is a brief, deliberate piece of choreography – my attempt to demonstrate to all those involved in this case that I'm not taking sides, that I'm talking to everyone, publicly.

"Hello, Englishman." One of the lawyers greets me in the same way, every day. And the point is never lost on me. I'm an outsider, a stranger poking around, trying to understand a community wrestling with painful divisions, secrets and suspicions. It has been a slow journey to win people's trust.

This story crept up on me, almost by accident. I first drove to Parys in early 2016 on a whim. It was a convenient hour and fifteen minutes from Johannesburg on an immaculate motorway. No harm in taking a look. I'd read a few local reports about the killings and the tensions in town but I was wary about delving into a subject that is so often boiled down to simple headlines about land and race. Us against them. I was looking for a subtler tale – one that could capture some of the deeper complexities and challenges of modern South Africa.

On the first day, I sat at the back of a crowded courtroom watching a young magistrate being openly demeaned and insulted by the prosecution. Soon she was pushed off the case. I saw how the two dead men and their families were unapologetically discounted – too poor to matter, except in terms of some short-lived political capital. And I saw the way one brief moment of fury was now rippling through the whole town, destroying not just a few individuals and their families, but threatening a whole community's fragile sense of harmony. I was quickly hooked.

In the years since the killings – a time period stretched and warped, far beyond the patience of all involved, by courtroom battles, delays and brinkmanship – I have visited Parys and Tumahole more than a hundred times. I've been to church services, funerals, shacks, micro-breweries, taverns, coffee shops, political rallies, bowling greens, government offices, and celebrations. I've explored the farmlands outside town, given interviews about my research on both local community radio stations, and ridden the white-water rapids on the Vaal

River. I've come to appreciate the town's quiet, often over-looked successes, its jarring failings, and the extent to which Parys may well be the nearest thing I've come across to a microcosm of South Africa.

My aim, from the start, was not to write a current affairs book, or a treatise on race, or land, or poverty, or politics. You will find no statistics, or broader analysis of the state of the nation here, and no reportage describing my own experiences and conclusions. Rather, I wanted to write a piece of narrative non-fiction, constructed entirely from the raw material I've gathered, enabling all those involved in a painful, tortuous tale to tell it from their own perspectives.

Over time, most of the key figures in the case agreed to speak to me. Some talked without preconditions. A handful spoke only on condition of anonymity. I recorded almost every on-the-record interview, took notes of more informal chats, and promised each person who agreed to talk that I would not use, or leak, or publish anything they said until the trial was over. Many people were extraordinarily generous and frank.

Turning "real life" into narrative non-fiction is an ambiguous conundrum that better writers than me have been wrestling with for centuries. The process comes with no clear rules but many risks and duties. I am acutely aware that, working in a country of such deep inequalities, I have a special responsibility not to abuse the trust, or presume to speak for, those who lack power or feel marginalised in their own communities.

I have chosen to use direct quotation marks only rarely in the book – most often when using court transcripts, recorded text and phone messages, and when describing events that I personally witnessed. Other conversations, comments and thoughts are drawn from my own detailed interviews but left without quotation marks in order to acknowledge the fact that they are based on people's memories, on first or second-hand accounts, and have been reconstructed and woven into a work that inevitably involves elements of subjectivity and even artistic license. As such they are fallible. But not deliberately inaccurate. At times I have chosen to write in a way that seeks to recreate the inner voice and thoughts of key characters. Again, these sections are based, exclusively, on my typed transcriptions, notes, and, on occasion, recollections of on-the-record conversations, interviews and statements – which collectively run to some half a million words. I have not sought to put my own words in anyone's mouth.

Early in the book, as you may remember, Ruth and Mercia stand facing each other in a farmhouse kitchen on the day after the killings – each with a fundamentally different, conflicting view of the situation at hand. For me, the scene represents what I'd like to think of as the book's heart, its unspoken chorus – a small reminder that in this inspiring, frustrating, fractured country, it is possible for two or more realities to coexist, to orbit each other, and that wounds – old and new – can only heal properly when we make the effort to recognise, and to acknowledge, someone else's truth.

ACKNOWLEDGEMENTS

Many people – only some of whom are named in this book – took the time to help, explain, correct and challenge me over the past three years as I meandered around Parys, Tumahole, and the countryside beyond. Mbulelo Mtshilibe was a wonderful translator and guide. The staff of Parys magistrate's court, Alet van der Walt, Mayor Joey Mochela, Sakkie van der Schyff, Steve Naale, Rian Malan, Saal de Jager, Graeme Addison, Bernadette Hall, Parys Hospital C.E.O. Ntabiseng Malinga, Jacques Steenkamp, Karen Schoonbee, Anthony Altbeker and many others were all generous with their advice and support.

I want to thank Christopher MacLehose and Katharina Bielenberg at MacLehose Press in London for their extraordinary enthusiasm, commitment, and patience, along with Corinna Zifko and the team at Quercus Books, my brilliant, incisive editor, Alison Lowry, the team at PanMacmillan in Johannesburg, my Dutch publisher Jan Gaarlandt at Balans, and my formidably persistent agent, Rebecca Carter at Janklow and Nesbit. My B.B.C. colleagues were once again kind enough to give me time off to work on a project that has taken far longer than anyone anticipated. A special thanks, not for the first time, to Becky Lipscombe.

Above all, I'd like to thank my family: my three sons, Alex,

Sam and Dexter, for indulging and humouring me once again; my sister, Clare Mather, for her comments and encouragement; and my wife, Jenny Hodgson, for reading all those drafts, for her judgement, and for making it all worthwhile.

ANDREW HARDING left London in 1991, aged twenty-four, and has lived and worked abroad as a foreign correspondent ever since. He spent a decade in the former Soviet Union before moving to east Africa and then to Singapore as the B.B.C.'s Asia correspondent. Since 2009, he has been the B.B.C.'s Africa correspondent. He has reported from numerous conflict zones, including Chechnya, Afghanistan, Iraq, D.R. Congo, Burma, Central African Republic, Mali, Côte d'Ivoire and Libya, winning many awards including an Emmy. Andrew is married, with three sons. He is the author of *The Mayor of Mogadishu: A Story of Chaos and Redemption in the Ruins of Somalia* (2016).